"F" The Housewives

Stop Watching. Start Living.

By

DeEtta Jones

"F" The Housewives
Stop Watching. Start Living.

Copyright © 2013 by **DeEtta Jones**

All rights reserved.

This book may not be reproduced in whole or part, in any form or by any means, mechanical, including photocopying and recording or by any electronic information storage system now known or invented hereafter, without written consent from the author except in the case of brief quotations embodied in articles and reviews.

SHARED PEN Edition

www.SharedPen.com

For information about the book go to

www.Fthehousewives.com

ISBN: 0615786529

Library of Congress Number: 2013935210

Inside Front Cover

"DeEtta and I have a long-standing joke — people don't know what they're in for just by looking at her. That warm smile and soft exterior are a mere veil for the powerhouse of a woman within. In the full 20 years I've known her, DeEtta has tirelessly dedicated herself to her work and making a positive impact on the lives of others."

Dr. Kevin Rolle, Vice President, Alabama A&M

"DeEtta's multi-dimensional take on life makes her the perfect person to write this book, and at the perfect time. She blends solid credentials with the voice and energy of today's generation of women and leaders."

Alicia Edwards, University Administrator and Multicultural Education Professional

"I've been calling DeEtta "the next Oprah" since the day we met. I have watched her bring a room to tears and then to a place of higher learning and inspiration. Her ability to quickly assess a group's need, customize her approach and create win-win outcomes for all involved, is masterful."

Jerome Offord, Dean of Library Services and University Archives, Lincoln University (MO)

"DeEtta Jones is a live wire! Her infectious desire to think big has helped many a young professional begin her own journey to authenticity. In working with her over the span of two decades, I have seen her create magic through her ability to connect with the needs of others. DeEtta's passion is to make sure everyone can achieve personal growth—whatever that may mean for each individual."

Kathryn Deiss, Association of College and Research Libraries Content Strategist

Table of Contents

Foreword	9
Dedication	13
With Gratitude	15
Introduction	17
Myths and Truths : Pop Culture Phenomenon and Reality Beyond the Hype	26
Part I: What Do You Want?	33
Chapter I: "Housewives" are Married to Ballers and Shot Callers	38
It All Begins With A Vision	43
The Power of Vision	45
Let Passion Guide You	80
Part II: What Can You Leverage?	85
Chapter II: "Housewives" Only Show the Glam and the Drama	88
Multi-Dimensional You	92
Mosaic of Diversity	98
Part III: How Are You Positioned As An Influencer of Yourself and Others?	114
Chapter III: "Housewives" Have Editors	118
Chapter IV: "Housewives" Have a Hair and Make-Up Crew	122
The Gift of Mentors…Danger of Anti-Mentors	128
Create Your Identity, Manage Your Brand	139
Setting a Positive Tone	144
A Word on Trust	146
Chapter V: Foolishness = Rewards *Only for "Housewives"*	148
Epilogue	160

8 "F" the Housewives

Foreword

From our initial meeting in Washington, D.C., DeEtta and I developed a deep personal friendship because the Universe conspired in our favor. We shared a natural attraction of energy that, almost magnetically, drew us together. She and I are both convinced that a greater purpose, beyond merely a friendship, underlies our connection.

DeEtta is the perfect person to author *"F" the Housewives: Stop Watching. Start Living*. She is beautiful inside and out, an intellectual with strong opinions, and has a vibrant personality that exudes the same sense of untamed fun and life-changing guidance foreshadowed in the title.

This book is the culmination of years and years of her life's work—DeEtta's own personal journey that has led to her growing influence on a global stage. As a person who has attended and experienced some of DeEtta's leadership sessions, I have witnessed her mastery of content and ability to, without a moment's hesitation, answer any question, complete with full citations. Her professional prowess is accentuated by her outgoing and unconventional personality.

In a world where we still tend to judge books — and people — by their "covers," upon first glance she seems too beautiful to be that intellectually captivating and driven, but don't let the red bottom stilettos fool you! Her unique blend of attributes is precisely why I asked her to be an expert contributor on my weekly radio talk show *Ask-Cherado*, which covers a wide range of topics from communication skills to romance.

DeEtta's segment is focused on giving advice to listeners about how to maximize personal and professional effectiveness. She listens as callers present problems and then skillfully engages them not only in problem-solving, but also teaches them techniques for mastering the problem solving process. She is a masterful coach and guide — possessing the magic touch that represents the strategic difference between giving a person a fish and teaching her how to fish.

But my intent is not simply to provide accolades for this author's considerable accomplishments. Rather, my special opportunity here is to testify to the strength and resonance of DeEtta's message through the lenses of another woman whose multi-dimensionality is worn as a badge of honor. I am a multi-racial Nicaraguan woman whose career has

spanned from journalism to real estate, and now I am a successful entrepreneur and media personality.

I am blessed to be married to my true soul mate, a man 15 years my senior who brought to our relationship two young children. Together we have added to our family a son, Cruz, who calls DeEtta "Auntie Dee-Dee."

Every one of my days is filled with the very juggling act DeEtta describes in the pages that follow. And every day I am thankful to have people like her in my life, reminding me to focus with intention on my vision and be fearless in its pursuit. It is with these principles firmly planted at the forefront of my mind — and reinforced by a village of friends, colleagues and advocates — that I have been able to build a successful path toward realizing my own vision.

The same principles that I use in my life and witness as central to the choices of other successful women are also those DeEtta presents in *"F" the Housewives*. As an author or a speaker, her voice resonates with women of any age group and from all walks of life, representing the full spectrum of social classes, as well as academic and professional backgrounds she encounters in her consulting practice.

All in all, life has been good to DeEtta and me. With love and family at the forefront, our challenges have required us to choose between simplicity and stability or multi-dimensionality and continuously evolving. She and I both chose the latter — and hopefully this book will encourage you to reflect on how your life's ambitions and goals are reflected in your daily choices.

Some of the obvious choices are called into question, such as family structure, career, and geographic location, and so are some of the not-so-obvious choices. These include examining how your own behaviors and friendship circles are impacting the way you are perceived by others and how your communication patterns are creating your personal brand.

DeEtta's book not only presents but walks you through the developmental journey that is the essence of every successful woman's story. In the process, she does not expect you to bare more than she herself exposes in the spirit of sisterhood and modeling.

It is my deepest hope that you will embrace this book for its light-hearted, timely and results-oriented approach to making a serious investment in the betterment of your own life. Like DeEtta herself, it has been a game-changer for me.

Cher L. Castillo Freeman

Owner, SKY Real Estate and Host of the AskCherado Show

Dedication

I dedicate this book to my parents, Jacqueline L. Jones and Floyd Jones. I know there have been times that I have chosen to judge. Now I am a parent and have so much more perspective. You gave my sisters and me everything you had and I am deeply grateful for all you have done. The only appropriate, yet insufficient, words I can give are *thank you*. I love and appreciate you.

"F" the Housewives

With Gratitude

Throughout this book I mention the role of significant people who have provided care and guidance for me along my life's journey. To all of you, named and unnamed, thank you. Every experience I have had to date has shaped me into the person I am now — and I appreciate each of your contributions along the way.

My sister Melanie Jones-Stewart and BFF Cher Castillo Freeman, thank you for being "ride or die" as usual — brainstorming ideas, reviewing drafts, and even flying across country to help me with the photo shoot. Susan Miller, you will never know how much I appreciate your giving me the directive, "Publish it!" and connecting me with Hedi Butler, who provided loving affirmation and helped bring my thoughts to life.

Jeff Shear, Nicole Magnum and Triphena Johnson, you made a camera-shy woman look and feel beautiful. Stacey Ferguson, thank you guiding me through this leg of my personal identity development journey. Kaylyn Groves and Carol Freeman, thank you for poring over every word and Carol, for the pep talk in the home stretch that brought tears to my eyes.

Thank you to my beautiful and generous friends who modeled for the photographs: Cher Castillo Freeman, Theresa Gorman (who also "loaned" us Holly, the precious pup on the cover photo), Rosy Hugener (also my publisher), Melanie Jones-Stewart, Sara McKinnon-Martinez, Linda Pascucci (and Joe, behind the scenes), Cari Sherer, Bridget Sevcik, Jennifer Uremovich.

The people who were most "put upon" by this book project are, of course, my family. You are the generous, unselfish souls who have listened to my endless chattering as ideas floated through my mind, fended for yourselves when I spent long nights on the computer instead of interacting with you, or taking on childcare duties as I scrambled to meet a deadline.

Mommy, thank you for stepping in as Grandma extraordinaire when I was in need of quiet time. You are always willing to help and only want in return the pleasure of watching your children find happiness. Daddy and my sisters Monya, Melanie and Monique, thank you for taking time to listen to yet another project I was pursuing while managing your own busy schedules and families. I can only begin to tell you how much I appreciate you. Kyla, Cyrus, Mary, Sarah and R.J., I'm so proud of each of you and thankful for your ever-present support and love.

Shiloh, my precious Gift-from-God son, thank you for being so happy and whole and bringing me peace. It is with those feelings flowing through my heart that I was free to pursue personal aspirations.

Finally, thank you Richard for loving me in spite of my time away from home, my hours and hours pent-up in the home office writing and re-writing, endlessly testing ideas and concepts on you. You have been my biggest supporter — bragging even before the first draft was complete. I love your faith in me; it makes me stronger and pushes me to excel. You make me better.

Introduction

As this book is being written, the United States marked the 175th anniversary of the Emancipation Proclamation, celebrated the 50th anniversary of the March on Washington where Dr. Martin Luther King, Jr. gave his iconic "I Have a Dream" speech, and inaugurated, for a second term, our first African-American President on the national King Holiday.

Watching a new chapter of living history unfold was heady stuff for all of us. Especially the bold agenda set forth to promote a more inclusive society where women, blacks, Hispanics, and gays — among other variously marginalized groups — can enjoy the social, economic and political equality promised to all Americans.

Make no mistake about it. Even with the enormity of the national challenges confronting us, women are living at a time filled with tremendous possibilities for personal growth. Some of us attach a now-or-never urgency to making things happen, while others are stuck in a holding pattern. There are just too many uncertainties, they moan.

These folks remain passively in the wings, unwilling or unable to take center stage in exploring opportunities to improve their own lives. Are you one of them? Well, you've got plenty of company and lots of distractions from pursuing your own goals. Particularly on those flat screens all over your house.

Today, soaring production costs have driven television networks to opt for more reality programming. Not surprisingly, seemingly sixty percent of the shows on television are now reality-based. Among the most widely viewed are those in the Bravo channel's coast-to-coast "Real Housewives" franchise — six current and former shows in the U.S. and more than 60 "Housewives" — that depict narrowly prescribed views of women's lives touted as glamorous and successful.

Millions of viewers flock to Bravo to watch often blinged-up, self-absorbed caricatures of "real women" — from Beverly Hills to New York City, New Jersey, Miami, Washington, D.C. (canceled after one season) and Orange County, where the "Real Housewives" debuted as a real-world response to the fictional characters on ABC's popular "Desperate Housewives."

While the lifestyles featured in some locales appear more authentic than others, many are simply contrived to lure more viewers into the fantasy. In any episode of the more upscale versions, cast members can be seen breezing through lavishly appointed mansions or chic high-rise condos, flashing red bottoms at top-tier eateries, rocking designer dresses at elegant cocktail parties, or just relaxing by resort-style pools. Life in these luxe lanes has become addictively aspirational for many viewers.

And let's not forget the "train wrecks," the dumbed-down "Housewives" who, despite their relative affluence, also draw in huge audience numbers simply by their bad behavior. Whether fiery tempers or thinly veiled jealousies drive them over the top, their catfights, including table flipping and wig pulling, keep the blogosphere abuzz with fans heatedly taking sides and joining the endless flow of back-biting gossip. Remember, cast longevity depends on who can and will deliver the most high-octane drama.

Could this factor have accounted to the early demise of the D.C.-based show? Despite the presence of Michaele and Tareq Salahi, the notorious White House gatecrashers, and the franchise's first black couple with two high-achieving non-celebrity professionals, was it still too tame to attract and sustain viewership?

Consider too that the reality spectrum includes magazines filled with teenage mothers, addicts in need of intervention and young children being dressed up as grown women, humiliated by a tyrannical dance teacher, or urging folks to "redneckognize." The country seems obsessed with "Kimye" and all things Kardashian, as well as Blue Ivy's reported $200,000 first birthday party. Keepin' it real? Not so much.

Let's face it, there are so many inputs with no end in sight. And new reality spin-offs are being launched every season. It's no wonder that entertainment masked as life gets so much airplay. It's mindless and easy to digest.

But here's the problem. We can only focus on so many things at a time. We have to make choices, prioritize. So in the midst of all of this noise the role I'd like to play is traffic director — encouraging readers to make intentional choices about who or what should get the major focus of your attention. I nominate YOU.

We must lift our heads out of the media fog, put down the remote control, and start living our own lives to the fullest. It is my fervent hope that my voice and message will resonate with you. And that this book will inspire a critical mass of women to build lives that are self-directed and filled with ambitious goals for themselves and in service to others.

This mission awaited the emergence of a new voice, even an unfamiliar one. I'm sure few of you have ever heard the name "DeEtta Jones" or seen it in print. Until the publication of this book, I have been able to operate largely below the radar of the publicity that accompanies a relationship with a high-profile partner or even the specialized professional context of my experience as a consultant working with thousands of national and international clients.

Why *this* voice? You see I have spent the past 20 years guiding people through the process of self-exploration and growth, teaching on topics ranging from diversity and inclusion to managerial effectiveness and leadership coaching. I have worked with multi-national companies, universities, not-for-profits — spending about 80 percent of my time away from home, delivering speeches and consulting all over the world to offer expert insight.

Why *now?* For years, I have been getting pressure to write a book that would make available to a broader audience the kind of information I routinely provide to my clients. But I have long wrestled in my mind with an appropriate "angle" for the book. I have plenty to say, but how might I package my message in a more accessible way that not only gives unique insight but is fun to read? Hmmm…

The answer came in an unexpected way. Just this past Halloween I was sitting around a fire pit in front of a neighbor's house sipping champagne with fourteen of my glamorous girlfriends, some draped in minks, and handing out candy. The men-folk were off in golf carts and Cadillac trucks taking our children trick-or-treating around our gated neighborhood. Got the mental picture? Between sips of the bubbly, one of the women said with a playfully wicked grin, "We are *so* the Housewives!"

Aha! Could this be the long elusive "angle" for my book? That night I went home, tucked the kids into bed and started writing. Ideas swirled around in my head. Admittedly, many of my friends and I do enjoy lifestyles that might be compared outwardly to those of the "Housewives." We are indeed blessed with material assets, as well as social and economic mobility that a lot of hard work — and yes, some good luck — have afforded us. But that is where the comparison ends.

We are also real women with real lives that are generally not camera-ready. Most of us have ongoing personal responsibilities for our families and some, like me, are working moms with time-intensive professional obligations. We face the demands of our own lives one day at a time. With perks, to be sure, but challenges remain. So few if any of us would be willing or prepared to have our lives filmed as entertainment, although there's probably great sit-com potential in many of our households.

In fact, the same spirit of good-natured fun that began on that Halloween night persuaded my girlfriends to agree to pose for the "Housewives"-themed photo that illustrate the final chapter title. But let me make it clear at the outset that this book is not intended as a put-down of "Real Housewives" casts across the country who have made that decision.

Rather, my premise highlights the far-reaching societal impact of their tremendous success: millions of viewers, primarily women, have become so captivated by watching their televised lives that they have become increasingly detached from their own.

I know the title may startle some, and the "Housewives" angle may be a bit off-putting for others, but the fact that you are reading the book feels like a victory to me. I took on this project knowing that it would be a huge personal risk, but one well worth taking if I succeeded in reaching just one person in a truly positive, life-altering way.

Let me explain. I am one of four children raised primarily by a single mother, a dedicated Jehovah's Witness who simultaneously worked two to three part-time jobs. Throughout my childhood I attended religious meetings three to four times per week *and then* went door-to-door on Saturday and Sunday mornings spreading the Good News of Jehovah's Kingdom to my neighbors and anyone else who would listen.

Not for lack of my parent's effort and desire, but my childhood was filled with tough times. I walked miles during those early years, holding my little sisters' hands for a free Thanksgiving meal. We even lived for short periods of time in shelters. But I was accepted into and made it through college by the Grace of God and the skin of my teeth. Despite the hardships and with no "pedigree" to propel my success, I have managed to enjoy a fulfilling life that has not only transcended the circumstances of my youth, but allowed me develop a unique voice that resonates with others.

By positioning myself at the juncture of preparation and opportunity, I landed some pretty damn good jobs that afforded me advanced educational attainment, global travel and experience, and platforms in the public and private sectors to stand and share my convictions. Yes, I have had a safe and successful career. I have worked hard. I have stayed in my lane. I have been the consummate "professional."

Well, now I want to be *me*. I want to say what I want to say in the way I would say it to my friends. I want to make up for all those years of never believing in Santa Claus or celebrating my own birthday because of our religious beliefs; for years spent working three jobs to put myself through school. I want to take the bun out of my hair, put on my sassy red lipstick and still deliver a credible message that resonates with you. I want to let you know that you are not alone; that your frustrations are shared by others and that we are going to find answers together.

I spend a lot of time picking the brains of other women, asking questions that allow me to compare my life to theirs and perhaps find patterns. More than any other area of inquiry, I ask women to share with me their secrets for managing the demands: being a mother, spouse or partner and being a professional. I am not looking for time management strategies, but the source of the emotional strength — and balance — that fuels the seemingly never-ending and often thankless tasks that fill their days.

Different women, of course, give me different answers. The one surprising constant I have found, though, is that all the women with whom I have spoken are quite matter-of-fact, even positive, in their descriptions. It is true that I am often speaking with a pre-selected group of women—those who have stable financial circumstances, or have recently been in a long-term relationship, women who have experienced career success. Throughout these circles of women, I have been unable to detect resentment or bitterness despite clear acknowledgement that "we live in a man's world."

As the multi-dimensional woman emerges throughout society, now is the perfect time for us to embark on this journey together. We are fortunate to have before us today diverse role models of accomplished women. Sheryl Sandberg, Facebook executive and author of *Lean In: Women, Work, and the Will to Lead,* models for us how women can explore our passions at work and at home while she connects us with others, like actress Reese Witherspoon, media mogul Oprah Winfrey, US Senator Barbara Boxer and former US first lady Laura Bush, who demonstrate how stretching for a goal and believing in yourself can pay off.

Michelle Obama, our extraordinary First Lady, is an Ivy League-educated lawyer and administrator from working-class South Side Chicago roots who brings authenticity, competence and grace to her historic role at the President's side and as Mom-in-Chief. Sonya Sotomayor, who came from humble beginnings in the Bronx, rose to legal and judicial prominence and became the first Latina Supreme Court Justice. And Tammy Duckworth, an Asian-American veteran and double amputee from the Iraq War who has worked in veterans' affairs, was recently elected as a U.S. Representative from Illinois. Their inspiring stories of struggle and triumph are instructive and resonant examples of how drawing on all the dimensions of our lives can be used to create a powerful brand and position ourselves for success.

However blessed or challenged, most women's lives can seem almost scripted. Work all day, go home, pick up kids, cook for the family, do homework with the children and get them to bed at a reasonable time. Then we work some more.

Frankly, we often need a break. And many of us find a kind of "guilty pleasure" in watching pop culture's latest depictions of other women's lives for public consumption. The "Housewives" franchise has since taken on a life of its own while we (even those who don't admit it) tune in with ratings-boosting regularity to see soap opera-style plots acted out by real folks all too often stuck in un-reality.

But I would violate every principle of truth-in-advertising if the title leads any reader to assume that I have chosen to present merely an in-depth examination of the "Housewives." Show by show. Cast member by cast member. Bloggers and reality niche magazines have that turf covered; maybe saturated.

For me, however, this platform offers an attention-getting marquee that will allow me to go beyond the televised drama to address the larger, more personal and consequential issues in real women's lives. Thanks to a perfect storm of timing, experience and opportunity, I have been able to add "author" to my resume. And have a little light-hearted, non-preachy fun along the way.

You are reading the first in a series of books focused on a particular sector of the personal development continuum. It is what I know and do best – and what I share with diverse groups all over the world.

My approach is grounded in research-based best practices and presented in a voice and style that appeals specifically to women.

"F" the Housewives: Stop Watching. Start Living. is about self-awareness—the necessary starting point in any personal development journey. This spectrum begins with creating your personal vision and goes on to positioning yourself for influence. Future installments will include developing a professional toolkit and navigating culture. The assumption in this series is that you:

1. See yourself on a journey. You are willing to invest in the intentional process of identifying and laying the groundwork for your life's goals.

2. Are frustrated with your current situation. You know you have untapped potential, unrealized dreams and need help clarifying your next steps, or feel stuck in a rut and desperately want to find a way out.

3. Want a different approach. You are seeking a new voice and style of presenting options and strategies that resonate with you.

Don't get me wrong. I love Stephen Covey, Jim Collins and Daniel Goleman — authors of some of the most influential contemporary literature on personal communication and business strategy. I have read everything they've written, draw regularly on their theories and practices, and often recommend their books to my clients.

But there's something to be said for style—and that's where I step in. As the research shows, and every woman knows, we like observing the style of other women and respond well when we find something that resonates with us. We appreciate the full range of attributes contained in another's package — their sense of style, personal likeability, resonance with message, similarities in life circumstances, as well as the strength and inner fortitude in the face of some of the same challenges you might encounter.

On the other hand, I'm not an "entertainment personality with an opinion," as are so many authors of the new wave of self-help(ish) books. The guidance that I share in this book is of the same caliber that I give to my clients, who include leaders of large and multi-national companies, some of the most influential universities in the world; people with PhD's and MBA's and MD's and impressive track records of their own.

So as you move through the book, remember that these are not my "best guesses" about the concepts presented, nor the practices needed to move you in your desired direction. Rather, these are research-based and real world-tested best practices.

With that said, the "Housewives" are the fun visual and framework for this book as reflected in the chapter titles. Why not? Clearly people are drawn to "pretty people living the glamorous life." And my own life and relationship with Richard Dent — my reality — do provide a unique personal perspective, along with my professional qualifications, to take this tongue-in-cheek approach to leadership.

Richard is an NFL legend and Hall of Famer. When he walks down the street people yell out, "What's up, Colonel!" or "Look, it's the Sackman!" He was the Super Bowl XX MVP on arguably the greatest team in NFL history, the 1985 Chicago Bears. For those who are not sports-savvy or are too young to remember, Google "Super Bowl Shuffle" and you will find a Grammy-nominated (really!) video[1] of him and his teammates in their full glory.

We love showing that video to the kids. They get a huge kick out of mimicking their Daddy rapping. And feel a little pride, too, in this fun part of his illustrious past.

On top of all that, creating this book was a blast! I have worked with amazing and talented people who helped transform me from a conservative grey suit-wearing, expertise-driven consultant into a full-blown "Diva CEO" with a whole new outlook on my identity and how I want to help you shape yours! So enjoy the fun pictures in the spirit with which they were taken — a tangible acknowledgment of a special milestone in my personal and professional transformation.

As you page through the book, I urge you to think deeply about where you are in your own identity development journey. What is your personal vision? What are your professional aspirations? What are you doing to move toward reaching your desired goals? Throughout the book I will encourage you to discover and hone your vision to become a fully vested agent in pursuit of your personal and professional aspirations.

The guidance I offer was born out of the adventures and challenges I have lived, many of which will be familiar to you, combined with nearly two decades of study and professional experience working with people to enhance their ability and readiness for leadership. *Housewives* is a reflection of my holistic thinking on personal and leadership development but filtered through a woman's lenses — more precisely, a woman of color with the U.S.-based context.

This is a significant factor because women and people of color deal differently with the issue of identity. It is a huge part of our journey, but it is not a topic that is explicitly built into most mainstream leadership development programs. So although the book takes a light-spirited approach, it aims to get at personal and leadership development issues in ways that are more resonant with women.

The framework of this book is based on the content most often requested by my clients and sprinkled with stories and conversations I typically have with friends. So consider this a conversation with your very own leadership coach who is willing to talk to you like a friend. It's designed for women who want to do more in this world than sit on the couch and long for the lives others are living. And those who feel that too much of their discretionary time goes to unproductive voyeurism and escapism.

Housewives was written for those in the earliest stages of their careers as well as seasoned executives and self-aware women of any age who want a bit of a laugh couched in a helpful message. You'll find accessibly presented information that is both relevant and credible, including practical "how to" tips wherever possible.

Above all, enjoy this book as a good read with substance and humor that will make you smile on our life-changing journey together. No "Housewives" allowed.

(1) As cited on Wikipedia, "The 1985 rap hit recorded by the players of the Chicago Bears known as the "Super Bowl Shuffle" instantly became a mainstream phenomenon. The single sold more than a half-million copies and reached No. 41 on the US Billboard Hot 100 making the Chicago Bears the only American professional team of any sport with a hit single. The song was also nominated for a "Grammy Award" in 1985 for best rhythm and blues performance by a duo or group, and eventually lost to 'Kiss.'

Myths and Truths: Pop Culture Phenomenon and Reality behind the Hype

After our Halloween night encounter, my friends and I laughed knowingly at the scenario that inspired the fateful remark alluding to our perceived similarity to the "Housewives." We could even have carried the let's-pretend moment further and acted as though a Bravo production truck and crew were about to drive up at any minute to film us for an episode of a mythical "Real Housewives of Chicago"!

Was there now any doubt that the "Housewives" had become a 'household word' (pun intended) — a mental shorthand for a way of life many find enviable — at least as shown on camera? Whether you're a casual, regular or even non-viewer of any of the franchise shows, they are inescapable in all media platforms — a pop culture phenomenon that resonates, positively or negatively, with women from all walks of life.

Lest we get too far down the path of believing the "grass is greener" hype that surrounds us daily, I've outlined a few discrepancies between the perceptions associated with the "Housewives" and the reality behind the hype.

Myth #1: The "Housewives" are housewives.

Actually, most of the so-called 'Housewives' aren't married, hence are not legally "wives." Some were cast without even having life partners or stable relationships, a fact for which simply being over-the-top with high entertainment value seems to compensate. Perhaps we'll call them "aspirational wives," such as Atlanta's Kenya Moore. Or those who went on to tie the knot while on the show; i.e., Bethenny Frankel, Cynthia Bailey and Kim Zolciak.

It is ironic, however, that the 'Housewives' franchise has taken such a significant toll on the real marriages among cast members that some now refer to the "Housewives divorce curse." As the *Huffington Post* [1] aptly put it, "How many 'Housewives' does it take to realize that reality TV is probably not good for your marriage?" The online pop culture chronicler went on to cite 17 divorces as couplings fell apart in front of millions of viewers and exposed the cracks in what is presented as reality.

What could have been uglier than the vicious and widely publicized divorce of Beverly Hills' Camille and Kelsey Grammar or most recently, Adrienne and Paul Nassif? In Atlanta, DeShawn and Eric Snow, Lisa Wu and Ed Hartwell, Nene and Greg Leakes (although they are currently "engaged" to be married again). In Orange County, original eight-season cast member Vicki Gunsalvon was one of the first to shed a long-time husband and start up a new relationship.

And remember the lovely successful black couple mentioned earlier who appeared on the short-lived Washington, D.C. "Housewives"? Well, realtor Stacie Scott Turner and her tech executive husband Jason called it quits after the show, while Cat Ommanney and her former White House photographer spouse parted ways during filming.

But divorce couldn't get any tackier than the dramatic split of the Salahis when Michaele ran away with a rock guitarist, a former flame, and ended their reign of on- and off-camera deception. Beyond the White House fiasco, theirs was a glamorous make-believe world that included a Virginia horse farm with an under-funded charity polo tournament and a family winery that was barely functioning under severe financial constraints. Yet they solicited Stacie's help to find them an in-town Washington residence (we're talking huge bucks here!) and accepted an invitation from the Turners to fly to Paris with them to attend a relative's music concert in Paris.

They portray the best of all worlds, or so it might have seemed to hapless viewers in other parts of the country. As one who still loves the time I spent in D.C. and experienced the exciting and sophisticated folks you can meet there as an upwardly mobile 30-something professional, I confess that had I watched some of those episodes, perhaps I would have felt some twinges of longing to be a part of that scene. Instead, I was working diligently on building my consulting business where I would soon become a part of my own "jet set" — flying to meet the international clients I had carefully cultivated.

And what about the incurable romantics among "Housewives" viewers who devotedly followed the storyline of Bethenny Frankel, a brash but entertaining natural foods chef and now "Skinnygirl" mogul who symbolized the independent and super-ambitious New York City career woman? Her unlikely relationship with low-key fiancé Jason Hoppy was a popular fairy tale that spawned a spin-off appropriately called "Bethenny Ever After" that focused on Frankel's marriage and impending motherhood.

Well, Bethenny and Jason — like so many of their peers — are now tabloid fixtures as they endure a very public and nasty divorce, including custody and support issues regarding their little daughter. Is there a "Housewives" marriage curse? Probably not. Just a sad reminder that few if any marriages could survive playing out "the days of your lives" in front of millions of your "closest friends" — viewers who would be far better served by nurturing their own relationships.

Myth #2: The "Housewives" have more money than you.

While there are "Housewives" throughout all of the franchises who enjoy indisputable affluence, such as Beverly Hills restaurateur Lisa Vanderpump and Adrienne Maloof, viewers would be surprised to learn that a good number of them are simply role-playing, projecting grander and more affluent lifestyles than they lead when the cameras aren't rolling. Some are leasing houses used, in effect, as sets for their television appearances, while others have actually lost their "homes" to eviction or foreclosure.

In one case, the "wife" was being supported by a still-married "sugar daddy," while another was dependent on legally encumbered support payments from her baller ex. So what you see from a "net worth" perspective among the "Housewives" often varies widely from their real bottom line.

When there is financial insecurity, the cast members are willing to play the game to the max — to "bring it" — to keep those Bravo paychecks coming. According to *Radar* Online[2], the big winners in the salary department are the "breakout divas" of their shows. And Teresa Giudic easily occupies that slot on the New Jersey franchise, the most watched of the "Housewives" shows with an audience of three million. Teresa, who is almost equally loved and reviled by viewers, takes home an impressive $600,000 per season.

Radar continues, "hot on her high heel are Countess LuAnn de Lessep and Ramona Singe of the New York City franchise, with $500,000 each per season. And Orange Country's Vicki Gunvalson capitalizes on her longevity with $450,000 per season.

Atlanta's "I'm Rich" home girl and longtime fan favorite NeNe Leakes, who now appears on NBC's "The New Normal" and has previously appeared on Fox's "Glee," is paid $350,000 per season for her larger-than-life antics and has accumulated a net worth of $4.5 million, thanks to her popularity with viewers. But NeNe endured lean days of rented houses and the reported bankruptcy of her then-husband Greg (and current fiancé) before she was actually able to have the financial security she flossed on screen.

While "Housewives" cast members can earn six-digit paychecks per season, their new fame often creates its own set of problems, judging from the number of bankruptcies filed on the show. While Teresa Giudice is the franchise's top-earner, she and husband Joe famously filed for an $11 million bankruptcy in 2009.

For many of them, including NeNe, the celebrity associated with exposure as a "Housewife" can lead to side hustles that actually pay the bills. Or not. Atlanta's Cynthia Bailey, a veteran New York model, opened an agency. Teresa Giudice has become a best-selling author of Italian cookbooks. Kim Zolciak became a one-hit-wonder with her party anthem, "Tardy for the Party."

The song was produced by singer-composer-producer Kandi Burress, who now has her own online show, "Kandi Koated Nights," where she promotes a line of adult sex toys that has attracted attention and, we're told, impressive sales. But Sheree Whitfield and Lisa Hartwell had failed fashion lines, despite built-in promotion through the show.

In a league of her own is Bethenny Frankel, whose strong entrepreneurial bent was displayed during her initial exposure on "Housewives." Despite some initial legal challenges, Bethenny's reduced calorie "Skinnygirl" beverage label has been a runaway success with a weight-conscious public and was sold for millions, along with her related products. Add spin-off shows and a talk show to her brand expansion.

The object lesson here is that while some "Housewives" fake it until they make it, none has actually succeeded without actually walking the walk of pursuing concrete goals. Those who put in the time and effort to succeed in their off-camera enterprises are rewarded by the promotional boost of being on the show. Others languish in wannabe-land. Just as in real life.

Myth 3: The "Housewives" are B@!ches.

I just threw that in there to get your attention. They are, though, guilty of some pretty bitchy behavior. Reasons for this behavior are probably linked to one of four things:

a. Staged by producers to increase ratings ("Sheree, start yelling and flailing your arms, then give Kim's wig a little yank.") But in her first season, Camille Grammar did a pretty good job of becoming the poster girl b@!ch for her imperious and alienating personality. When it was revealed that her behavior was largely motived by the private hell of being dumped and cheated on by her actor husband, by the next season she became a cast and fan favorite. The take-away here is that another woman's perceived bitchery may have nothing to do with you and a little compassion could be in order. But the producers loved it and it still dominates plot lines, particularly in Atlanta where newcomer Kenya Moore has highly dramatic beefs with practically all her castmates. Like Teresa Guidice on the New Jersey show, being the "Housewife" all love to hate guarantees longevity. And ratings. So those who want to stay, play. And viewers should not be taken in by the drama of manipulated cat fights.

b. Editing that accentuates certain characteristics in one person versus another (e.g. Taylor's constant crying or NeNe's colorful put downs of all but her chosen few) in order to create distinctive roles for each of the ladies. Brandi Glanville has secured a place for herself as the resident "loose cannon" in Beverly Hills who boldly spews out uncensored remarks to keep things hot. Lights, camera, action!

c. Personal choices of the "Housewives" to secure popularity of their individual roles and continued success of the series. (Bye-bye D.C.!).

d. Delusions of grandeur. Some of these ladies go on to internalize their hyped personas and really think they "are" all that. And why shouldn't they? We tune in faithfully and watch them, buy their products, talk about their foolishness. They're invited to celebrity functions and walk the red carpet. They are tabloid staples and people fuss over them the same as actors, singers and athletes, although most of them have invested little if any of the hard work and dedication associated with those accomplishments.

Myth #4: The "Housewives" are Role Models.

No way! Role models are people you should intentionally choose to influence your thinking and choices. These ladies are living their lives, doing their thing. Let them do it. Even feel free to enjoy watching them do it. But insert intentionality into your own life. As you page through this book, think about all the ways in which the Housewives' personas do not match the vision you have for yourself. And if you have yet to establish a clear vision for yourself, read on.

(1)January 25, 2013

(2)December 19, 2012

"F" the Housewives

Part I: What Do You Want?

What do you want?

What can you leverage?

How are you positioned as an influencer now and in the future?

This section of the book — and of your journey — focuses on the foundational question: "What do you want?" I have provided a conceptual backdrop that will assist you in answering this question for yourself with deeper insight. The construct includes an imperative that you form a personal vision, accompanied by a compelling description of what purpose a vision serves and examples of how visions have fueled greatness in others.

Next, I will invite you to reflect on and begin to document your strengths and passions. Definitions for both are provided, as well as self-reflection questions to help you begin to formulate responses that are meaningful and actionable. By the end of Part I, you will be ready to begin the next leg of the journey.

Before we go any farther, let me tell you a bit about this process that I refer to herein as "journey." It's your life's journey. It's the journey that will help you decide who you want to be and what path you follow to get there.

We all have a journey. For me, the early stages of my journey started with trying to grapple with my own racial identity in a world that was still racially divided. I remember as a young girl riding in the car with my parents on a trip from Chicago to Arkansas for a family funeral. The police pulled us over and took my father to the police station—detaining him for being a black man married to a white woman. I remember my mother and her brother getting into arguments in our family home and hearing my beloved uncle call my mother a "nigger lover."

As an adolescent, I experienced race riots at my junior high school. I can still hear the voices of of kids taunting me with threats of physical harm if I did not declare a "side." I grew up in the 1970's and 80's, long before the popularity of Halle Berry, Mariah Carey, Alicia Keys, Tiger Woods and other famously biracial celebrities emerged . To compound the problem, I lived in an area well known for its pervasive racial segregation, even to this present day.

But race wasn't the only issue on my mind. I was also poor, practiced a religion that was largely misunderstood and negatively perceived, and was a pretty and shapely girl who attracted the unwanted attention of older men. By the time I got to college, I was confused, angry and misguided. I stumbled through the first half of my undergraduate years—nearly failing out of school.

By year three of my undergraduate experience, the Universe decided I had had enough. Perhaps it was time to direct me on the path of my true calling—to turn the hardships of my life to date, coupled with my insatiable desire to live a happy, full and rich life, into something meaningful beyond myself. This is the point when I began to study. I picked up every book I could find, on any topic. The distractions of my tumultuous childhood had left me without having read the foundational books that other undergraduates already had under their belts.

So I read those classics first: *Catcher in the Rye, Beloved, Of Mice and Men, The Scarlet Letter, To Kill a Mockingbird*, and on and on. Those books opened up new worlds for me through the eyes and sensibilities of some of our greatest storytellers across genres and generations. Then I took a course in African-American History. My professor, Dr. Blane Harding, was magical. At the same time, he was incredibly intelligent, down-to-earth and compassionate.

Blane (so down-to-earth that encouraged his students to use his first name instead of "Dr. Harding") didn't judge me harshly for having poor study skills. Instead, he challenged me to develop and demonstrate my fuller academic potential. As a biracial man himself, he invited his students to talk about the atrocities of racism and the healing power of education and ally-building. He acknowledged that some of us felt rage and others felt shame, and he walked us toward a better place, a healing place.

As I previously noted, this part of my life was fully in the hands of the Universe, which now seemed to be conspiring in my favor. That African-American History course was followed by several other significant and life-altering introductions to concepts and people whom I will mention throughout the book. But the concept that became the bedrock of all subsequent study for me was power. I became a student of power and continue to see myself in that way.

I needed to understand why I felt oppressed and what my options were for moving beyond being a victim. Next, I needed to understand how power worked within groups—how do groups lose or grow or abuse power?

Oppression became the next topic of my obsession. I wrote my graduate thesis, with considerable guidance from Blane, on Internalized Oppression and Shame Theory. Internalized Oppression is the turning of oppressive beliefs and behaviors inward, inflicting them on oneself and one's own group. Some readers will make the connection to the late Brazilian educator, Paolo Freire, who wrote brilliantly on this topic from an African Diasporan perspective in his landmark study, *The Pedagogy of the Oppressed*.

As the impact of my studies took hold in my own life—bolstered by exposure to the best research and thinking on the subjects—I was ready to share my hard-won insights. I began to teach an undergraduate course on identity and positioning oneself for success, specifically for African American students in a predominantly white campus setting. We talked about internalized oppression and how it played out in the black community. Then I entered a master's program that heavily emphasized counseling and cross-cultural communication.

The counseling courses undergirded my work as director of the human rights office, where so much of the expectation was to listen, educate, represent those who were often voiceless, research and mediate difficult conflicts to resolution. With these far-reaching responsibilities, I had to have more than just a conceptual knowledge base. I had to prepare myself to be able to make a real difference in people's lives.

So I focused heavily on turning my knowledge into specific skills and immersed myself in leadership literature. To this day, I am a voracious reader of everything leadership-related—strategy, influence, communication, self-awareness, motivation, team development. I went on to receive an MBA with a concentration in management. I regularly attend intensive training sessions and have also acquired certifications on the administration of self-assessment tools, creating and using scenarios to position companies, even industries, among others, for unknowable futures.

Luckily, I was able to combine my academic studies with my professional passion. Everything I learned was immediately translated from concept to tool that could be applied to solve a client's problem. But one struggle persisted throughout my career; finding literature and models of leaders who look like me and share some of my life experiences.

Although such sages do exist among people of color, the vast majority of those I encountered were white middle-aged men. I advocated from the outset of my career that diversity awareness, cross-cultural competence, management skill and leadership development must be one and the same. There is no other way to achieve the global perspective and practical know-how that will be required in an era of changing U.S. demographics reflected so profoundly in the last election.

My professional portfolio, as well as solid reputation for being fiercely committed to learning and always applying the highest standards to myself and my work— led to every leadership position I have held to date, and secured every client engagement. I have built my career on being able to bring to life the representation of a new voice of leaders— one that is multi-dimensional, credible, prepared and approaching life just a little differently than those on whose giant shoulders I stand.

---

(1) bell hooks, Alice Walker, Maya Angelou and Toni Morrison were larger than life contemporary figures of strength and multi-dimensional identity from the very beginning of my personal journey, and remain so today.

Chapter I

"Housewives" Are

Married to Ballers and Shot Callers

Housewives Are Married to Ballers and Shot Callers

...or come from wealthy families or have titles like "Countess" or some other attribute of social prominence. Not! This title was actually acquired by New York's LuAnn DeLesseps from her former husband, a legitimate Count, but "Countess LuAnn" managed to underwhelm many of her castmates and viewers as insufferably pretentious. She turned out to be a middle-class woman from Connecticut who attached her identity to a titled fantasy.

While the pedigrees of some "Housewives" display dramatic upward mobility, now divorce-wealthy Camille Grammar, a former background dancer early on in her career, persuaded her high-profile husband Kelsey to form a production company that is now flourishing with shows like BET's "The Game."

Across the franchises, the actual ballers and shot callers attached to "Housewives" as their sole providers are nearly matched by those women who can make legitimate claims to success fueled by their own enterprises and ambitions. Many of them were mentioned in an earlier discussion of the finances of the "Housewives."

With the stunningly high divorce rate uncoupling many of these unions, along with bankruptcies and other destabilizing factors, the era of the "Housewives" as modern-day Cinderellas supported by men of substantial means may be drawing to a close. While Atlanta now boasts two current and former NFL husbands, Kim Zolciak's Kroy Biermann of the Falcons and Porsha Williams Stewart's spouse Kordell, former Steelers standout and now ESPN analyst, others were not so lucky.

But while trophy wives and "arm candy" partners still prevail throughout the franchises, it can be legitimately said that despite the hype, many sisters of all hues are indeed doing it for themselves. From high-rolling Beverly Hills' businesswomen Lisa Vanderpump and Adrienne Maloof, along with ATL-based entertainment attorney Phaedra Parks and model agency owner Cynthia Bailey, cookbook mogul Teresa Guidice in New Jersey, and New York's Heather Thomas, former Beyoncé stylist and designer for the star's family-own clothing line, now owns a company that manufactures a line of Spanx-like undergarments. Roles are being redefined, even in reality genre hype, and the lap of luxury no longer comes from sitting on a partner's lap to achieve your own success and financial independence.

Yes, my better half (I like to call him "my better three-quarters") is world-class athlete Richard Dent. My identity, however, is not rooted in his success. I met Richard years ago when I was in Chicago on a business trip, already the owner of a consulting practice, a holder of multiple degrees and global business experience. As a matter of fact, one of the few major challenges in our relationship was my concern that his fame would overshadow and cast me into a "she's with him" category, distracting from the significant effort I have put into my self-development.

I do not take for granted the perks that come into my life because of my relationship with Richard. (You may have picked up this book because you recognized him on the cover.) But it is unmistakably clear — women are now coming into our time.

Evidence of this shift abounds. Around the world companies are investing heavily to ensure gender balance on executive boards, in the C-Suite positions, and to develop their pipeline of women who are ready to take on additional leadership responsibility. This comes as no surprise. There are more women in the workforce with higher-level skills and credentials than ever before. In addition, women's role in influencing markets is becoming clearer. We make significantly more than half of purchasing decisions in a household *and* we willingly share information about our favorite things with others. Think of it like a formula,, using Oprah Winfrey as an example:

Oprah's favorite things

X

All your BFFs

X

The Internet

***Huge* Market Impact**

If we are happy with a product or service, we tell everyone we know: at work (15 people), within our personal circles (36 people), on Facebook (500 people), LinkedIn (350 people), Twitter (3,000 people). Then we ask our friends to pass it on. Ladies, we have indeed come into our own time.

And since it's our time, let's figure out exactly what we're going to do with it. My hope and professional advice is that we should step into the momentum that exists around us. That means you should create and pursue your own vision, build on your own strengths and use your own unique voice with the goal of creating a brand that positions you for influence.

It All Begins With Vision

For years I have been working super-hard at my career and my personal life. Since childhood, I have always felt a bit unconventional, as if I had a special talent but didn't have a name for it or a clear picture of how I fit into the world around me. I stumbled through my undergraduate years, chose my first graduate degree program based on availability of assistantships, and wandered into new experiences that would eventually turn into my career.

But I was wandering through life. My actions weren't intentional, focused on a specific achievement or the accomplishment of a clearly defined end goal. That's how it is for a lot of people. It's called drifting — drifting through school, relationships, jobs, life. That's how it's been for me, at least.

For many years, I made choices based on what I didn't want — in a job, in a workplace environment, in pay, in a man, in friendships. It's not a bad tactical approach, but it's limited. I took as many steps backward as forward, constantly repositioning and hoping to find a more comfortable place for myself. After years of effort, the most I have ever got was greater certainty of what I *didn't* want, which left me feeling incredibly unfulfilled — always wanting more.

This "wanting more" state is painful. It's like death by a thousand cuts. It is also a very popular state of existence for a lot of people, and women in particular. We settle. We have a little whisper in our ear — coming from our gut or the Universe — that gets ignored, even suppressed.

We experience slight insults — I call them "nibbles" — [1]at work about our communication style, our style of dress, our credentials. We experience little nibbles from our friends—subtle comments about our weight, our career stall, our choice in a partner. We experience little nibbles from family members—guilt-laden messages about our priorities. Yet day-in and day-out we continue to invest in these relationships and hold our tongue.

We look around at our friends, sisters, colleagues and rationalize, "My life is like so many other women." Or "What I'm feeling is just a woman's burden to bear." We give ourselves mental pep talks about being thankful for the good things and remembering those who have it far worse than we do.

We are accustomed to feeling moderately overworked and underappreciated. We acknowledge that we're living in a man's world. All the while we want more, you want more. You know you have more inside of you than you have accessed thus far. If this speaks to you, it's time for a change.

All change starts with a vision. A vision is a vivid and compelling end state — an aspired-for destination. Vivid means that you should be able to close your eyes and see the vision in detail, including seeing yourself in it. A compelling vision is one that is so enticing that you cannot help but act in a way that brings it into being. It is powerful enough to stimulate energy that makes you literally jump out of bed in the morning, or stay up all night, or do whatever it takes to make it become reality.

(1)Inspired by a book by Kaleel Jamison, <u>The Nibble Theory and the Kernel of Power: A Book About Leadership, Self-Empowerment, and Personal Growth</u>

The Power of Vision [1]

In the absence of a compelling vision people tend to focus primarily on fear — the "what if's" associated with not having a clear sense of the future. The energy used is called distress, or negative stress. Stressful energy is what we use to worry. We worry about paying our bills, worry about our kids' behavior, worry about the tension-filled relationship with our colleague, worry about why our man isn't more attentive. As you know, this kind of energy is emotionally exhausting.

Here's something else worth mentioning. The human brain is wired so that when we feel fear manifested in forms such as stress, worry, threat or embarrassment, a part of the brain called the *amygdala* triggers a cortisol release into our bloodstream. The cortisol then redirects resources from the analytical, problem-solving, thinking part of the brain to the extremities — our arms and hands, legs and feet. It puts us into the primal "fight, flight or flee" mode, which is the survival-oriented wiring humans have had for thousands of years.

It was practical when we were running from bears or warring clans, but it's a little less useful in modern times when running from a stressful or embarrassing situation is typically the least useful response. Nowadays, having access to the analytical, problem-solving, thinking part of our brain, *particularly* in fear-filled situations, would be much more helpful.

Think of the last time you had a disagreement with your boss, or colleague, or spouse. Do you remember how you felt? If you had an argument, think of what you said at the time, then *what you wish you had said* after having some time to reflect on the exchange. Isn't that how it goes — two days later you're standing in the shower and exactly the right words come to your mind?

That's because the immediate threat has been removed. Your emotional state then levels out and the fullest resources go back to feeding the rational, creative, problem-solving part of your brain. It is important to understand this cortisol release in response to input that elicits fear because we are bombarded daily by stimuli that can trigger our amygdala.

> *Eustress—the creative energy needed to bring something new into being.*

Think back again to the argument you had in your mind a few sentences ago. What happened directly after that argument? What did you do next? Did you have another unpleasant experience? It's likely you did. Do you know why? Because the cortisol that was released in your body from the first argument takes two to three hours to wear off. In the meantime, your amygdala is a hair trigger. The next minor infraction is just adding the proverbial fuel to the fire emotionally speaking. It's why you go from having a bad experience to having a bad day. Familiar? It explains a lot, doesn't it?

So here's an important thing to remember. As humans we are wired to have emotional responses. Emotion is not a bad thing, it just *is*. In fact, we have emotional responses to a stimulus before we have rational ones. This is why marketing specialists focus on which colors or scents elicit an increased propensity for buying and what kind of background music playing in a store is most likely to lessen the inhibition to spend money.

In fact, it explains why I chose a title and image that would jump out at you. Emotions are powerful — in either direction. Emotions that focus on fear are powerfully able to cause distress. Emotions that focus on vision are powerfully able to stimulate *eustress* — creativity, the energy needed to bring something new into being. So there is hope for better management of our energy. We can shift our focus to vision.

Close your eyes and think about something you have created in the past. It can be anything at all — a database, a cake from scratch, a website, a business, a child. Now remember the process of bringing that new thing into being. Was it challenging? Painful at times? Did you stretch beyond your comfort zone? Were you in constant learner mode?

Now think about the outcome of your efforts? When you look at your creation, how do you feel? How do others feel about it? How do others feel about you after witnessing the effort and the outcome? My expectation is that those of you who actually thought about a personal creation and the outcomes associated with it are feeling a bit of a tingle right now.

Those are the emotional memories that humans bring forward when we recall something we did that made us proud. I think about my son. Whew, that was some work! I recall being eight months' pregnant and walking in the winter across an icy bridge from one building at the University of Minnesota to another. I remember standing and delivering a two-day workshop at the New York Public Library exactly one month, to the day, after having a C-Section.

I remember the sleepless nights that were my constant reality during his first two years. I think about the temper tantrums and emergency room visits. And every day I look into his face with the greatest feeling of satisfaction and love possible. I have grown as a person, felt the fullest range of human emotions — fear, anxiety, impatience, gratitude, pride, extraordinary love — because I had a vision of being a great mother.

That vision is still so compelling that I jump out of bed every day and do anything necessary to make it come into being. The energy used to fuel pursuit of a vision is called eustress, and it's good stress. It's the kind of stress that produces positive feelings and a sense of fulfillment. The feeling is not associated with the stressor itself, rather how the stressor is perceived, which changes depending on positive feelings such as control or healthy challenge. Eustress allows us to feel meaning or satisfaction or hope as a result of our effort.

Think about this for a minute. Once you have identified a vivid and compelling vision for yourself then you can use the positive energy produced through pursuit of that vision to fuel your continued effort. (A bit of foreshadowing: this is related to intrinsic motivation and will be covered in the second book in this series, which focuses on developing a leadership toolkit).

Now think about your current reality. What does your life look like right now? Is it calling for a massive overhaul? Is it mostly good but could use some strategic choices and actions to get you out of drift mode and onto the path of your vision?

Listen. If you need to make a significant change, please don't just make a mental acknowledgement. Say it out loud. Don't just say what's not working. Let's use this as the moment to shift from the negative to the affirmative, from focusing on fear to focusing on aspiration.

What do you want? Close your eyes. Do you see it? Is it so compelling that it will catapult you out of bed tomorrow morning? If not, you still have some work to do. If so, get going. Start telling people, anyone who will listen, about your vision.

Of course there will be naysayers. Ignore them. Listen to their dissenting points of view so that any insight that might be present in their comments is considered on your journey, but do not let them slow you down. Heck, let the naysayers speed you up, give you a bit of ammunition. Let this be your moment to show 'em what you got! That's what I did.

This book was a huge risk for me. On one hand, let's call this the professional hand, I had a stable career based on a carefully-honed image and reputation that I have been building for nearly twenty years. My steady stream of clients came without me even having to market my services. I took on every request, always did more than was asked, always asked for less than was deserved, and often swallowed my pride by taking on tasks that were menial compared to my actual skill set.

I did this for almost two decades because in my head I kept telling myself that I should feel thankful for what I have; that especially in this economy, I need to realize that others have it much worse; and most of all, I accepted that reality because I didn't have a vision for what I truly wanted for myself. I just knew what I didn't want – and that was to be a failure and broke.

On the other hand, my personal hand, I had a relatively young relationship with a celebrity athlete. Walking into his life and identifying myself as his girlfriend was a bit painful. I wish I had a dollar for every time I have been introduced as "and guest" while walking arm-in-arm with Richard.

I have had experiences with his long-time acquaintances making comments that are hurtful, all the while disguised as compliments. "Oh, we like you so much more than all the other women he's brought around in the past." Or a guy friend whispering to him after first being introduced to me, "You sure go through 'em." Even the wives and girlfriends of ballers and shot callers have to lay their heads down at night and make peace with their existence.

Richard and I know our relationship. We know our own history of ups and downs and how grateful we are to be together. We understand that we are a team. But it's still tricky to find a place for my identity, my ego, my vision to shine when I often feel overshadowed by his.

So this book, with the two of us on the cover and poking fun at what is sometimes a very difficult behind-the-scenes reality, is a huge risk. I am putting myself and our relationship in front of the world to see, and judge. Huge risk is required in order to make huge change; and this change is in the service of my vision.

When I told people in my professional circles about the concept for this book I got less than encouraging feedback. One person said point-blankly: "You can't use 'F' in the title. It will ruin your brand!" Another group of women read the rough draft and told me to drop the reference to the 'Housewives' altogether; that it took away from my credibility as an expert.

What if they're right? What if the dean of the prestigious university I've had a relationship with for years severs my contract because I published a book with reference to an obscenity in the title? Oh well, the photo shoot was done and paid for by the time I received that feedback. However, both of the aforementioned comments kept me up tossing and turning at night.

At any other point in my life, out of fear, I likely would have stopped working on the book, considered it an ill-thought out concept and hopped back on my hamster wheel. The difference for me this time was the vision. I could see the book sitting on a bookstore rack. I could imagine the cover photo and irreverent title catching a browser's eye among the dozens of other new releases competing for her attention.

My vision was so crisp. It spoke to me. I was able to hear the criticisms, think about whether or not I should make changes to the book concept based on the criticism, then re-focus on my vision realizing that sometimes my vision is just that, *my* vision. It's okay if everyone doesn't see it at the same time as me.

I often lead sessions where I ask participants to envision the characteristics of their organization, and the environment in which it exists and competes, in the future. Almost without fail, I get a perfect picture of today. It's difficult for the brain to think in leaps; it's wired more for incremental steps. This is the reason for spending time on this topic in this book, and for creating self-reflective exercises for you to complete along the way. These are the tools for helping you get from understanding your current reality to articulating a vision, which I have found over the years to be too amorphous an undertaking for most people in the absence of a clear and structured process and guide (like me).

First Assess Your Current Reality

In preparing to create your own vision, it's critical that you begin with an honest assessment of where things are today – your current reality. All of us have a sense of what's going on inside and around us: what's keeping you at a job you're not crazy about; what triggers your late night refrigerator raids; what your intimate relationship "feels" like at this moment. Many of us do not, however, think about those things systematically; that is, within the same context.

Further, we may not think about them often enough. Perhaps you, like me, think about the area of your life that is giving you the most discomfort at a particular point in time. You then turn more attention to complaining about and/or fixing that part of your life. Once the issue has resolved itself (which never happens) or you have fixed it, your attention shifts to another area of your life that demands immediate attention.

Resolution of creative tension can be accomplished by diminishing vision or by changing reality, but since reality tends to change faster than strongly held aspirations, holding the creative tension will likely move current reality toward vision (the power of intention).

You are careful not to look back to the previous area for fear that some untended remnant of the previously dealt with problem will reappear.

But I am going to propose a different approach, a periodic and more holistic analysis of your life's landscape. We experience changes in our lives regularly: new job, new title, new job responsibilities without a new title, new apartment, new boyfriend, new ex-boyfriend, new 10 pounds on the scale, new "must have" shoes, new level of anxiety because the bank account is so low, new idea, new attitude (sometimes bad, sometimes good). You get it.

Things change. It's important to look at your life's situation regularly because the changes often occur without our pausing to understand their implications, as well as potential opportunities afforded us by these changes. The worksheet on the following pages will allow you to begin looking inside and around you, and then make some notes about the current reality of your life. Avoid listing overly broad answers — drill down as much as possible so that the answers are meaningful for you, and specific enough to allow you to refer to them as you begin constructing your vision.

In the spirit of modeling I have included an example using my own answers given my current reality as of the date I am writing this portion of the book. My answers are very honest and personal. Your answers need not look like mine. Make yours reflect, honestly, your current reality .

Understanding Your Current Reality Worksheet
DeEtta's Example

Questions	My Answers
1) What 3 areas of your life currently demand most of your time?	Work: • Travel 2-3/week, work 10-14 hours/day x 5 days/week plus 4-5 hours/day on weekends • in addition to above, read 1-2 work-related books/week Caring for 5 and 8 year old boys—when I am home, I spend every moment with them in order to make up for the time I am away. Writing book/working on branding materials — requires quiet time to write and edit, Internet searching, correspondence with strategist, editors, publisher, etc.
2) What informs these priorities?	My desire to be independent, reliable and responsible heavily informs all three bullets. The first bullet is a reflection of my 1) need to maintain a stable financial base personally and for my business, 2) work ethic, but more so my 3) desire to remain in demand and not lose my edge. A mixture of love and guilt are probably the most honest answers for the second bullet. If I didn't have guilt, I would incorporate a bit more "me time" into the equation when I'm not traveling for work. The third bullet is informed again by a desire to not lose my edge, as well as a belief that the marketplace is changing fast and I need to catch up or get left behind.

3) What life changes did you make in the past 12-18 months to respond to changing to these priorities?	I haven't changed my work schedule, though I have been "planning to" since the birth of my son. I hired a new nanny to help me feel a bit more secure about the boy's care given Richard and my demanding schedules. I took several trips with Shiloh to build in one-on-one time. I wrote a book draft, then contracted with a brand strategist, publisher, editor and photography team to begin putting the wheels in motion. Assembling the team put the additional pressure on me to actually finish the book—and give me access to needed support.
4) What changes are you planning to make within the next 12-18 months? Why these? How are you deciding upon these?	Professional: I am planning to launch a new website and a book, including significant marketing around each. These are important because they will allow me to broaden the base for my business, and experiment with other business ideas and potential collaborators. Professional: I plan to increase the amount of time spent on the Make a Dent Foundation. This is time-sensitive because of the new projects being led by the Foundation. Personal: I plan to get involved with the local theater community. As a newcomer and an arts lover, I want to become more closely connected with the Chicago community. Personal: I am going to once and for all "F" the Guilt! It's weighing me down .
5) What are some of the factors outside of your control that will influence your ability to make the above-mentioned choices?	The boy's developmental needs. Richard's willingness to support me, even give me a boost, in making media connections and through difficult times (which also takes into account his own considerable project load). My health—I find myself sick or emotionally and physically exhausted with some regularity. My house in Washington, D.C., which seems to need expensive repairs more and more often. This money could divert from other projects.

Understanding Your Current Reality Worksheet

Questions	My Answers
1) What 3 areas of your life currently demand most of your time?	
2) What informs these priorities?	

3) What life changes did you make in the past 12-18 months to respond to changing to these priorities?	
4) What changes are you planning to make within the next 12-18 months? Why these? How are you deciding upon these?	
5) What are some of the factors outside of your control that will influence your ability to make the above-mentioned choices?	

After completing the *Assessing Your Current Reality Worksheet* look back over your answers. Reflect on what you wrote. Are your answers specific? Are they addressing the most important parts of your current reality? Are your answers honest? Let me restate—an honest description of your current reality is needed. It's impossible to create an accurate roadmap to your vision unless you can identify a beginning point.

Once you are comfortable with your understanding of current reality—pause. How do you feel when you think about it? A bit frustrated? Anxious? Anticipatory? Great! Let's move ahead.

(1) Inspired by Robert Fritz's Structural Tension Model

Practices to Increase your Propensity for Visioning

You are now ready to turn your full attention to vision. I know that visioning as a structured process is new for a lot of readers. To do a bit of foreshadowing, the third book in this series will focus on understanding culture and leading change. In that book, I will describe in detail how to create and use scenarios as a powerful organizational positioning tool.

Scenarios are also helpful in one's personal life. Scenarios are, in short, plausible stories about the future that allow us to make strategic choices ahead of time; that is, to approach choices proactively rather than in response to some undesirable change in our current realities. Scenarios are possible future current realities that sit alongside your vision. It's important to anticipate possible scenarios for the future as they will have an impact on your vision.

Let me share with you a painful example, but one that drives home the importance of scenaric thinking. In 2009, my 33-year-old friend Greg tragically and suddenly died. He left behind his five-year-old daughter Madison and wife Lanaya, who was four months pregnant. I had seen Greg just days before his death. He walked into a party at a friend's house, smiling from ear to ear because he had just that day received the news that his unborn baby was his long anticipated boy.

Lanaya was a careful planner and insisted that they wait until after she finished her medical residency before having another child. She wasn't at the party because she had taken a train to New York to celebrate passing her meexams. This day was the perfect storm for both of them. They were young, happy and at a pivotal turning point in their lives.

Lanaya was finally ready to begin practicing medicine after years spent in medical school and residency programs, all while living primarily on Greg's income and raising a young child. Greg was finally going to complete his family and be able to loosen his belt now that Lanaya would have more sizable income as well. Three days later Greg was gone and it felt like the whole world turned upside down.

We had a nickname for Greg — "P.I.P." for "Party in a Person" — because he was so full of life. I had never met a happier person. In preparation for Greg's funeral, I wrote a letter to his unborn son, now named Austin.

September 26, 2009

Dear Baby Smith,

I already know your name — your Daddy told me a few days ago. He was so, so excited about your arrival. He's been "wishing out loud" for you for years. There's a part of me that agonizes about him never getting to meet you, nor you him. But another part of me — the part that is closest to understanding God's will—knows that you are his gift to your mom.

Your Dad was bigger than life. His personality was magnetic. EVERYONE LOVED HIM! In the years that I've known him, every memory I have of your Dad is happy or funny—every single one. Please know that you're surrounded by people who loved him, and love you, and will help you come to know him through us.

One of the most adorable things your Dad ever did was take Madison trick-or-treating last Halloween with Ms. Karen, Adam, Uncle Enrique and Shiloh—just them. I was out of town on business. Your Mom was working. So they got together with the children and went to the mall to trick-or-treat. Your Mom has the pictures. She'll show them to you. He was looking forward to taking you trick-or-treating — already talking about it and your Mom's only four months pregnant!

Your Grandma Brooks told me, "Greg never met a stranger." That was so true. He could make friends with anyone. Every time we all got together Greg would invite people we had never seen before. He would say, "Oh, that's my friend so-and-so." We'd ask how they knew each other and he'd say, "I met him yesterday in the grocery store" or something like that. He just met and befriended people. He and your Uncle Enrique are birds of a feather in that way, which made them like brothers from the day they met.

I look forward to knowing you and helping you know your Dad. Just imagine that the silliest, most gregarious parts of your personality — those characteristics come from him. And your Mom, she's so strong. Your Dad depended on her strength for years. He admired and respected and was deeply in love with her. He's looking down on you now, with loving eyes and wishing he could be here to love you in person the way he loves you from heaven.

With all my love, Auntie DeeDee

Scenaric thinking would have pushed Greg and Lanaya to think, separately and as a couple, to imagine the "what if's." Of course, such thinking would not have decreased the amount of pain and suffering felt by Lanaya or any of us who loved Greg. Instead, its purpose would have been to inform conversations about possible future realities and contingency plans that may be put in place, in case the worst occurs.

Just to give closure to this story, I am happy to report that Lanaya is a successful practitioner at the renowned Johns Hopkins University Hospital in Baltimore, MD., and her children are happy, healthy and loved. Greg is indeed showering them with his love from heaven.

Another practice that is much easier to digest involves shifting our focus from tactical to strategic approaches. I have a sister who is a manager for one of the largest security companies in the world. She hustles 24/7. Her phone is constantly ringing, or she's preparing and presenting financial summaries, reprimanding wayward employees or wooing prospective clients. She's always looking for more hours in the day, and when they're found, she fills them with phone calls and performance management meetings too.

My sister describes her job as "putting out small fires." That statement probably resonates with most managers, most mothers and in most of our lives. It's not bad to spend time putting out fires, but it's tactical. All you have at the end of the day is a fire avoided and something that didn't burn down.

I challenge you to reframe your existence — now, today. Focus less on, though not completely away from, what you *don't* want and more on what you *do* want. Dream in an unedited way, push yourself outside the lines. I am not suggesting that you quit your job to pursue a dream and just hope that it will come into being. Though I do recommend that you practice reframing your approach to life in ways that limit your risk but still allow you to reap significant personal benefits.

Using my own life as an example, I have for years complained about my demanding schedule and lack of work/life balance. I travel frequently and have limited time to spend with friends, at the gym or pursuing a hobby. I would look around at other professionals who were setting and accomplishing non-work-related goals and make excuses about why I couldn't be like them.

"My job is different. It's more emotionally draining," I'd tell myself. Or I'd rationalize, "Well, she *is* busy but at least not on planes all the time. The travel is my extra burden to bear." Then one day I was having a conversation with a colleague who had just run a marathon. It's true, she didn't travel as much as I did, but her job did require a fair amount of travel and a lot of managerial responsibility. She was incredibly accomplished and productive professionally. "How did she do it?" I wondered. "I would love to run a marathon. That would feel like a huge personal badge of honor."

Duly inspired, I set out to run a marathon. I found an organization in town that trains people using a tested program and as part of a team. More important, runners raised money for HIV/AIDS education and awareness, an issue that is very near and dear to my heart.

On the first day of the group run we were to take a running test—three miles. "No sweat," I thought. By the end of the run, however, I was limping and miserable. I went home and tried to imagine how a person like me could ever run a marathon. Over the next week I forced myself to put on running shoes and begin the agonizing march, only to circle a block or two then head back to my hotel room.

My determination was wearing down and I just couldn't see my way to becoming a marathoner. Then it hit me — marathoners are runners. I was a person trying to force myself to run. I needed to *become* a runner. I needed to name and then own a new aspect of my identity. I am DeEtta Jones, a runner. Even better, I am DeEtta Jones, a marathoner. Because I am a marathoner, running must move from the *optional* category in my brain to the *not-optional* category.

Marathoners run. Run, DeEtta, run. And I did. I ran. And I repeated the little mantra in my head every step of the way, one mile at a time, 26.2 times. In this story, tactical efforts are the individual miles. Strategy is the marathon. Strategic efforts are in pursuit of a larger goal.

You may be asking yourself, "Where do I begin in creating a personal vision?" Do something simple and tactile like creating a vision board. Get a poster from a crafts store then give yourself the gift of finding a happy and serene physical space with plenty of room on the floor to spread out. Put on some uplifting music and start paging through magazines. Imagine all that you want—only affirmative thoughts should be in your mind.

> *"Because I am a marathoner, running must move from the optional category in my brain to the not-optional category."*

Dream big. Stretch yourself. Do not limit or edit your imagination. Do not pause to give yourself reality checks. Do not consider what you now believe is plausible or likely. Just dream. Look for images in the magazines that represent the images in your mind. Think about your whole self—your spiritual self, your professional self, you as a mother, daughter, sister, friend, colleague, mentor, protégé. Think about yourself as a community leader, the member of a congregation, a team member. Imagine your aspired-for physical self. What size clothes you are wearing? How do you feel in your own skin? Imagine what you would wake up looking at every day. Imagine how you would spend your ideal day.

How do I get from concept to practice? How do I get from my current reality to an actionable path that allows me to draw on my creative energy?

Creating Your Vision

On the subject of developing a vision, leadership expert Stephen Covey describes, beginning "with the end in mind." Realizing your vision can only happen after you have honed in on it. In the spirit of practicality, I am going to guide you through a three-tiered visioning process. This will allow you to anchor high (e.g. your storyboard) then dig in deeper around specific aspects of your life that will need focused attention if your vision is to be realized. This will be the basis of your solid action plan that separates thinking from action.

Visioning Exercise: Tier I

Instructions: Answer the questions below as thoroughly as possible.

1. What do you want to achieve in your life?

    Here's a fun exercise I sometimes use with clients: Imagine that you are being featured on the TV news for your accomplishments. How would the journalist describe you and your achievements?

2. What do you stand for?

3. What are you willing to sacrifice to reach your goals?

4. What values do you hold sacred?

5. Reflecting on your answers to questions 1-4, write your personal vision statement. It should be 2-5 sentences that capture, to the extent possible, the highest level ambitions you have for yourself holistically.

Insert Your Vision Here

Visioning Exercise: Tier II

This is where you dig deeper. Focus on one area of your life and answer the follow questions. For purposes of example, let's choose your career as the area that you'd like to flesh out. Note: You can repeat this same exercise for multiple areas of your life.

1. What are your career goals for the next five years?

2. What is your near term career timeline? Where do you see yourself in 5 years?

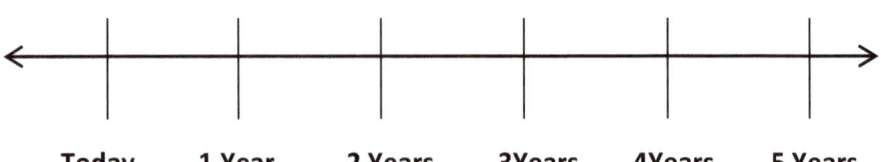

Today   1 Year   2 Years   3 Years   4 Years   5 Years

Now don't get overwhelmed by the numbers. Time flies when you're chasing your vision, so it won't be that difficult to plot out how you see the next 20 years of your career.

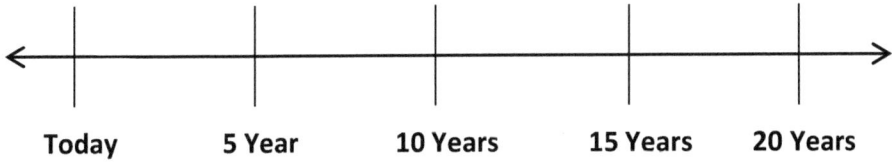

3. What are your career benchmarks that you review, monitor and update? In other words, how will you know along the way that you are on the right path? These benchmarks will allow you to make needed adjustments along the way.

4. What specific professional skills you will need to master to achieve your career goals and personal vision?

5. What leadership competencies will you need to develop or enhance?

Visioning Exercise: Tier III

This is the stage where you translate the information you provided in Tier II into concrete goals. After identifying those goals, describe what you will need to gain (knowledge and skills) and change (mindset and behaviors) to achieve those goals. Finally, give yourself a date. The date may need to be changed because of something in your environment over which you have little or no control, but start with a firm "accomplished by" date in mind. This will ensure that the specific action steps you take feed into the short- and long-term timelines that you outlined above.

Visioning Exercise: Tier III - DeEtta's Example

Goals	Knowledge Needed	Skills Needed	Mindset Change	Behavior Change	Accomplished by
To have a best-selling book by 2014.	The requirements for "best-selling"	Writing	From "I don't have enough time to write a book" to *"Writing a book is not optional"*	From "work, work, work for clients" to "work for self (on book) *and* work for clients"	Book written by February 2013
	Leading edge concepts to present	Instructional design		Make a habit of *every morning* turning on the computer and *allocating at least 60 minutes to* working on the book, use time on planes to write and edit.	Begin conference appearances in March 2013
	Understanding of how to package leading edge concepts for popular demand	Marketing and promotion	From "How can I compete in an already overly crowded marketplace" to "I have exceptional skills and a unique branding concept that's sure to make this book a best seller"		Secure major media spotlight by July 2013
		Public speaking			

Visioning Exercise: Tier III - Your Turn

Goals	Knowledge	Skills Needed	Mindset Change	Behavior Change	Accomplished by

I hope the Visioning Exercise was been helpful in stimulating your thinking, and providing structure to begin on your path. Before going any further, let's talk about one of my favorite sayings and life lessons, given to me by none other than my own personal life coach, Richard Dent.

Do You!

I used to be in a marriage that felt like I was wearing somebody else's clothes; like the life I was living just wasn't quite the right one for me. I struggled during the entire marriage to put my finger on exactly what was wrong. I was ignoring that internal alarm that we all have and instead, listening to society's constant messages that made me feel I should be married to be complete.

I didn't know what to do. I took up yoga, immersed myself in new projects, started seeing a counselor, even cut off all my hair (like maybe a new haircut will quiet the Universe's screaming in my ears!). Well, my marriage eventually ended, I moved to another state and through the process I gave myself space to reflect and think about what makes me happy.

Like many of you, I am always so busy taking care of others and fulfilling obligations that I don't take enough time to reflect on my own needs. I came to the realization that I was living according to other people's expectations of me and their judgments. I had been making choices for my life based on other people's criteria and society's traditional expectations for women, which has always been too small a box for me to live in.

I vividly remember explaining all of this to Richard whose response was simple and perfect, "Dee, just do you." He went on to say, "Whatever that is, do it, wear it, let it shine. That confidence wins the day."

Amen! I think that most people have the potential to achieve this level of confidence but it has been pushed way down inside of us. As soon as we can find a way to build it back up and wear those pieces of our-

> *"Dee, just do you...*
> *Whatever that is, do it,*
> *wear it, let it shine.*
> *That confidence*
> *wins the day."*
>
> *- Richard Dent*

selves that are truly us, that truly allow us to express ourselves in our own unique way, dress the way we uniquely dress, smile the way we uniquely smile, wear our hair the way we uniquely wear it, whatever it is, then our identity will truly have a chance to shine.

Embracing, nurturing and learning to leverage your individuality is such an important component of having a successful career and a balanced life. One of the things I love most about my dearest friends and colleagues is that they are able to be wholly themselves; they embrace the things about themselves that are interesting, even if kind of quirky.

"Do you" is really about feeling comfortable in your own skin. I think it takes people time to feel comfortable in their own skins, but there are some lucky people who seem to be born this way. My friend Cher is one of these people—she oozes and radiates confidence in a way that rubs off on me.

People enjoy being around her because she, without saying as much, honors the "you" in "do you." As for me, even though I've believed it and preached it for a long time, I think that I am still getting comfortable in my own skin and deeply appreciate people like Cher and Richard, and others whom I have purposely sought out and placed in my life, for helping me grow my "Do you" capacity.

Expressing your truest self is much more of a journey for some of us than it is for others. It is especially hard for people who come from marginalized groups, including poor people, young people or people who grew up in dysfunctional environments.

I am biracial and my family spent time in shelters and on public assistance during my childhood. My mother is shy and lacks confidence in many social situations and she supplied the vast majority of messages I received in my youth. As I mentioned at the beginning of Part I of this book, I stumbled into my career as part of my own identity development journey—seeking to understand who I am separate and apart from the world around me. Regardless of your story, don't let negative circumstances in your past or present become obstacles that you can't overcome. **It takes time, reflection and a lot of courage to "do you."**

Remember that all aspects of our lives are interconnected like a tapestry. No matter how hard we try to compartmentalize them, the pains that exist within one area of our lives will affect other areas. Similarly, the joys and strengths that we cultivate in one area are able to stimulate growth in other areas.

People who have loving relationships, successful careers and are spiritually and emotionally balanced aren't actually born that way; they've worked at it. Just as I stated earlier that we should all be in networking mode to capitalize on opportunity at any time, we should also constantly nurture our true nature.

How? First, schedule time to be self-reflective and escape the noise that surrounds you, even the noise in your own head. A little selfishness used to help you focus and establish clarity is healthy beyond measure. Begin to listen to the voice inside, that feeling in your gut that tells you when something is right. Ask yourself, "Is this me?" Am I where I should be—emotionally, physically, spiritually, professionally, etc.?

Find a friend who exhibits the kind of confidence that really resonates with you and practice it. Practice wearing your own skin and feeling comfortable. Start at a social level and then move outward. Think about the friends you surround yourself with, the things that you watch on television, the kinds of books you read, the experiences you have in the workplace or the people you are asked to mentor.

You may realize that some of these relationships force you into situations that are counter to your true self. Do not be afraid to make changes. You may need to disassociate with some friends or change jobs. Energy feeds energy. Positive energy perpetuates positive energy. Negative energy perpetuates negative energy. Every thoughtful change you make positions you to have a support system that enables confidence-building experiences.

Learn and Leverage Your Strengths

People have varied interests and experiences that shape their paths. Identifying and then leveraging your strengths is a key component in developing yourself. How do you know your strengths? Here's the formula:

$$\frac{\text{Natural Talent}+ \text{Enough Interest to Commit to Ongoing Practice (Passion)}}{}= \text{Strength}^{(1)}$$

Most of us are born with some natural talent, whether or not we have fully maximized it is another story. For now, think about the things that you are naturally good at: are you athletic? Are you good with math? Are you a strong writer?

Next, what do you enjoy doing enough that you are willing to spend your time investing in getting better at it? What is it that you do for sheer enjoyment even if it does not pay your bills? Your strength can be found where the talent and the interest intersect. As long as I can remember, I have always possessed a great deal of internal drive and optimism. Through all adversity my outlook remains positive and I always feel that I can overcome whatever I am facing.

These are innate qualities. They were not adopted from family or mimicked from others. It is a part of who I am. Being in tune with this inner voice and listening to it allows me to recognize my strengths. My inner voice plays a major role in my decision making process. Certain qualities are a part of our characters. I do not fully understand how mine developed but I recognize the existence of these characteristics and use them as a compass and stabilizing force in my life.

I am 5'6" and camera shy. Sometimes I wonder if I am camera shy because I'm never satisfied with pictures of myself or the other way around. Either way, I've never been willing to spend too much time in front of a camera because it's agonizingly painful for me to try to figure out how to pose. Do I smile or not smile? What do I do with my hands? Is the person with the camera ever going to take the damn shot? And my bottom line is that I know I am going to be disappointed with the photo anyway.

When I was about 15 years old I was scouted to model. Of course I was thrilled and flattered, and enthusiastically started taking classes and putting together a portfolio. I loved runway work and went on to do a few local shows—every time with me as a major contributor. At some point, though, my instructor sat me down for a heart-to-heart.

"You're pretty, but in a cute girl-next-door sort of way. Your features aren't unique, pronounced or distinctive. On top of that, you're too short to go any farther with runway. It's time you turn your energy to print and television."

Imagine my disappointment. The only option I had for pursuing my then dream was to focus solely on work that required me to be in front of the dreaded cameras. That was it; my modeling aspirations ended that day. I didn't have the innate ability (or qualities/attributes) for runway nor the interest (or confidence/desire) to potentially increase my camera presence. I just didn't have what it took to turn modeling into a personal strength.

What are the take-aways from this story? Well, for me, I could have sought another opinion. The person who advised me was one person with one opinion. If my interest had been stronger, I probably would have consulted with more people about my chances as a model. Other opinions, or a strong supporter, may have led me to invest the time and energy needed to become more comfortable in front of a camera.

I mean, look around now. How many 5'6" women with features not altogether different from mine do you see on the covers of magazines, in movies, as new anchors, etc.? So here are the Take-aways from this story:

1. Don't sell yourself short.

2. Before you go self-assessing your strengths and making life-altering decisions based on your own skewed self-image, get feedback.

3. Sometimes an aspiration really isn't and won't ever become a personal strength—maybe an interest or a hobby or a dream, but not always a strength. Know when that's the case, too.

What are your strengths? What are those innate characteristics that you possess that will contribute to success? What added value can you bring to your clients, company or job? Often it is easier for us to identify someone else's strengths than it is for us to recognize our own. Friends, peers and mentors can serve as a barometer for helping to gauge your strengths if you are having difficulty pin-pointing them.

My friends and I refer to each other as the "The Crew." They are a group of very talented individuals with a range of careers and strengths. The crew consists of attorneys, business owners and professionals, a techy, a doctor, a professor and me. Individually, these people all know who they are and are comfortable internalizing and owning their strengths.

They're incredibly confident women who aren't competing with one another, aren't judging one another, aren't pulling or putting each other down. As a matter of fact, we go to great lengths to hoist each other up. To a person, everyone in the crew is strong, positive, constructive and filled with confidence.

We consult each other at the personal and professional levels and never hesitate to provide feedback that will promote helpful awareness and growth. At various times several of us have collaborated on projects and they are a good sounding board for ideas. I value these friends and their opinions so much not only because each of them is dynamic and accomplished but because they are honest. When I seek out their feedback, I know always that it comes from a place of good intentions — even if it is hard to swallow.

Like my group of friends your "crew" probably recognizes talents in you. It's empowering to have people who know you well and are willing to give you honest input. Draw on their friendship more deliberately, engaging them in your self-development plan.

As helpful as the input of friends and mentors can be in developing your strengths, draw also on other sources to gain insight about your preferences and get data about the impact of your behavior. Try tools like self-evaluations, which can be formal or informal. For example, an informal evaluation could be as simple as a journaling exercise where you answer the following five questions:

1. If I could choose any career for myself, and money were not a factor, what would it be? Why?

2. I am regularly praised when I _____ ?

3. If I had to write a personal essay in 5 words, what words would best capture my essence?

4. If I could take a 6-week course on any subject, I would choose _____ .

5. I feel most proud of myself when I _____.

After you have answered these questions for yourself, ask a trusted friend or mentor to have a discussion with you. Share the questions in advance and ask her to come to your meeting prepared to share her answers to the same questions about you. Discuss the similarities and differences in your answers. What conclusions can you now draw about your strengths? Are there any areas or answers that surprised you? If so, then you should look more into how you are being perceived.

Some people, after a bit of self-evaluation, feel frustrated. "My strengths aren't the right ones! I want her strengths!" If this is the case with you, don't become discouraged. Although we are wired with aptitudes for certain things, **through conscious effort, we can also grow ability in areas we find lacking or desirable.**

For example, optimism is something I've worked hard to grow in myself. I've always felt that being optimistic is an important characteristic, but I had very few role models in my youth who demonstrated it, and even fewer experiences to make the case for it. Yet, inside my gut I've always longed to see the bright side of things, to know that possibilities exist beyond the often callous reality I was living.

Early in my college career as a psychology major, I found literature that corroborated my hunch and that was based in science. I started reading books about optimism specifically, and then about the mind, and then about the impact of emotions on performance. I learned that optimism could be increased through mental re-framing exercises. To support my efforts, I sought out friends and mentors who were optimistic and listened to them talk.

I reflected on their choices and on people's corresponding response to them, which were almost always affirmative, then mimicked their language. I did this for many years, and still do quite often. My point, of course, is that once you identify the key ingredients you want to be included in the recipe for "you," you can grow in areas that you may be naturally lacking in the desired quantity.

The next step after determining your strengths is figuring out how to leverage them. Leveraging strengths is the movement from acknowledgement to action. Anthony Robbins, the personal peak performance guru, says that people are motivated to change for one of two reasons: inspiration or desperation. To that, I say "Amen"!

If you're reading this book but you have no reason to actually *do* anything differently or believe that no severely negative or rapturously positive result will come from your concerted effort, the chances are slim-to-none that these words are a call-to-action for you. If this is the case, enjoy the pictures. But I do hope you will pick up the book again when you've hit a wall. It will resonate more with you at that point.

In 2005 my company went through a major strategic planning process and I learned that my position and the positions of the people I supervised were to be eliminated. That hurt. I had devoted nearly ten years of my life to that organization, gone to graduate school two times to try to keep up with their standards, traveled around the world—coach class—to scrape together money to meet our cost-recovery budget needs and they were going to eliminate us! I was angry and scared and, even worse, I felt guilty for not being able to make a strong enough case to preserve our division and ensure my staff's positions.

My response was not unusual. An emotional response typically comes first, before a rational one, when we feel threatened or fearful. (Remember the amygdala?) Over the next several months, I worked through my emotions to find rational options and the ability to have calm conversations with my colleagues.

I facilitated exit plans for my staff, re-deploying one person within the company. Then I negotiated for myself a contract that allowed me to have some ongoing income while I figured out what to do next. I used this time to think about my own interests and possibilities, imagining what other types of work I might pursue.

Somehow I got the real estate bug and decided to get a license. After earning my real estate license, I bought a house, my first and last transaction as an agent. Interestingly, I met one of my dearest friends during this time. She was a young real estate broker and helped me find the house I would buy on Capitol Hill, two doors away from her. This friend whom I've already referenced, Cher, would introduce me to a whole village of friends, people I would have never known left to my own introverted devices.

As cliché as it sounds, it's true: the interesting thing about life's journey is that you never know where it will take you. Here's my professional urging — be open to the journey but begin by defining what is really important to you now. I'm all for serendipity, but the odds are that you'll find more positives than negatives if you explicitly look for them.

I haven't always known exactly where my career was going to take me in terms of what job, what title, what city. But I've always known the sorts of things that I'm attracted to and that make me feel whole and motivated individually. I knew real estate wasn't for me by the end of the first class. But entrepreneurship was important to me and that's what I was actually drawn to when I signed up for that class.

I like freedom, flexibility, autonomy, feeling like I am in charge of something and that I have the ability to make decisions. I also like to be challenged; I like to know that I am putting myself in a situation where I have to work really hard and that the stakes are high if I don't perform. Your turn: Reflect on your own touchstones. Not knowing exactly what you will find under every stone along life's path, what do you hope to find?

This Is the Time of the Creative People

The workforce is shifting, expanding in some ways and contracting in others. Employers are looking for people who are technically and interpersonally skilled—competent with a "can do" attitude. Working for the same company for 20 years is a thing of past generations.

Now we are combining educational disciplines, skills and interests into interesting personal portfolios that position us less for a particular job and more for a type of contribution. Tapping into and taking ownership of your individuality allows you to think creatively about how you brand yourself professionally, and market that brand.

Richard Florida, urbanist and author of the bestselling book *The Rise of the Creative Class*, talks about this newly labeled group of people who are able to draw on the analytical and the creative aspects of themselves and fuse them together.

Different from dreaming of being a lawyer or an engineer, the creative class includes those with law degrees who are also musicians or engineers with fine arts degrees. These folks combine right and left brain strengths into unique combinations and bring the result—unique perspectives and expressions—to the workplace and marketplace. Their boundaries are further blurred by new and emerging standards for working, as contractors, consultants, and even telecommuters across continents.

For those of you who are at a crossroads, you've been downsized or right-sized or displaced, I challenge you to expand your definition of yourself professionally. Think about not the box you came from, but the arena within which you want to play. It is not a waste of time to pursue that philosophy or art degree you have had in the back of your mind for years. Disregard old conventions, reassess and sharpen your skills with the next generation in mind. Understanding how the land-

scape is changing applies even to making decisions about child-rearing. For example, the expectation from many is that Richard (Dent) and my boys will play football. Our decision has been to focus on helping them develop a broader base. Shiloh is four years old and has yet to attend a Bears game, but he has been taking piano and Spanish lessons for a full year. We want to develop and encourage their creative pursuits along with athleticism and other interests that they will develop on their own.

Although we are already in the time of the creative class it is difficult for many of us to break the old mindset. My parents' generation saw themselves as developing a trade that was going to get them through their careers. People still in the workforce need to reset their way of thinking. It would be absolutely detrimental to assume that one career is all you will have over the course of a lifetime instead of seeking a multifaceted development of skills and talents.

With this approach you may not know how or when these skills are going to tie in, but you will be ready when opportunity knocks—and when the next "new normal" emerges. It's not about advanced degrees—though I'm a huge advocate—but constantly nurturing your capability and love of learning. Explore your intellectual curiosity; study new languages, struggle with teaching yourself complicated games, engage in competitive activities. Teach your brain how to learn and never stop pushing your limits.

Be open to things that are not your pre-disposition. I am not good with numbers and much more of a conceptual rather than analytical thinker, so I got an MBA. It didn't transform me into CFO material, but it pushed me to grow in an area that would have become a career de-railer for me without some basic skill level and academic credentials. In other words, my goal in pursuing an MBA was not to turn a weakness into strength but to make sure that I did not let a weakness get in my way. By pursuing and earning the degree I have enough ability to be able to deal with numbers, make smart business decisions and negotiate contracts. Multifaceted development is an ongoing part of life.

Stop Watching Other People Live Their Lives—Go Get Your Own!

My D.C.-ness kicks in at this point. Although I now live in Chicago, I have spent most of my adult life in Washington, D.C., surrounded by people who primarily come from other places to do something interesting—to contribute. Many of the people who have come to D.C. over time have been born of privilege or were privileged enough to live comfortable high-society lives, or worked diligently for years to have an impact on an issue.

Eleanor Holmes Norton, Delegate to the United States Congress representing the District of Columbia, falls into the latter category of the issue-driven doers. After creating a name for herself in local politics, she could have skated on her popularity. Instead, she and other people of conviction and drive chose to work hard and distinguish themselves from their potentially overshadowing better halves through the strengths of their own talents, abilities and personas. (I think here of names like Clinton and Kennedy).

When I lived in Washington, I was blessed to find a whole group of women with similar qualities—women with strong identities, rich personal and professional lives, and positive values and mirroring behaviors. These are people who chose and are choosing to live their lives rather than watch others' from the sidelines or from the couch.

These are the people who are eagerly working to create a society that flourishes with small businesses, provides health care, fights for the underdog, makes sure affordable housing is available to average citizens, and promotes the love of art and culture within our communities. These are the kind of people who view relationships as an ecosystem, where giving and receiving are equally important and nurturing. Understanding, first-person, the personal power that comes from claiming agency over my own life, **I urge you, Dear Reader, to put down the remote control and go find the thing that excites you to action.**

Let Passion Guide You

One of my favorite words in the English language is "aspiration." As a consultant, I use it often when talking about topics like organizational vision and the powerful role of leaders. I tell clients that aspiration is that which we seek to become; that aspiring to reach a desired future will compel us to behave in ways that brings that future into being.

I am often sought out to provide insight about how best to break into personal and organizational consulting. When this happens, I am forced to think about the link between practical and theoretical aspects of my work, the requirement to understand human psychology and complex organizational systems, the ability to learn about a person or organization quickly yet deeply enough to provide thoughtful analysis.

More personally, it makes me think about myself as a consultant who often feels exhausted and overextended. Why do I continue to choose for myself a life that is more difficult than it would be if I were to make easier choices? Or do what many a friend has suggested and "let Richard take care of" me.

I am passionate about my work and see it as tied to my identity. I'm passionate about discovery—discovering pragmatic solutions for my clients, and discovering hidden potential within myself. That passion fuels the dogged pursuit of my personal and professional aspirations. How do I reinforce the importance of dogged pursuit of one's aspiration? The words are nice; they may even leave you with a momentary warm-fuzzy. But what I should emphasize to you is that aspiration must be fueled by a kind of personal zeal for achievement of a vision, an end state of being that is more compelling than where you are today.

This book fulfills a huge part of my personal and professional vision. While I have written book chapters and given speeches for years, I have never authored a book. I have great admiration for people with the blend of insight, credibility and discipline needed to get through such an undertaking. But it took me years to finally feel like "I had" to write a book.

My business had been rolling along pretty well for years, and then I had a son. As a consultant with a far-flung roster of clients, I was on the road more than 80% of the time. Not to mention creating highly-customized experiences and materials for every client. I was exhausted, mentally and physically, and feeling guilty about the time away from my child.

On top of everything, I went through a divorce and had to face tough new single-woman realities: healthcare, child care and my own retirement. I hit rock bottom, a desperate emotional place that was fueled by my fear about the sustainability of my current practices. Fear, I realized, is unproductive. It's stress-inducing and kept me filled with anxiety rather than creative energy.

I forced myself to re-focus my energy away from fear and toward my vision, or at least a piece of my vision of becoming an author. I forced myself to let my aspiration be the anchor to which I attached feeling rather than fear. That's the good thing about anchoring to your vision, a high and personally compelling vision – it forces action. It is so enticing that you can't help but behave in a way that brings it into being.

In a blog post by Rosabeth Moss Kanter entitled, "Does Your Passion Match Your Aspiration" she nails the concept in a very accessible way. Kanter, a guru in the fields of leadership, change management and organizational development, says, "Leaders who create extraordinary new possibilities are passionate about their mission and tenacious in pursuit of it. Many people have good ideas, but many fewer are willing to put themselves on the line for them. Passion separates good intentions and opportunism from real accomplishments."

We should be more explicit about integrating the expectation of passion (as in popular advertising taglines promoting the "passionate pursuit of personal excellence" or "passionate about delivering the highest quality customer experience") into our personal goals or organization's strategic planning and change processes. This sort of passion is what I think we mean when we talk about "achievement", "fulfillment", "accountability", "customer service" and "engagement."

The acknowledgement of passion in pursuit of our goals or company's mission is more powerful because it wells from an internal source of motivation. And its intent and impact are key to securing commitment. Now reflect, what ignites your passion?

Re-Igniting your Passion: Exercise

Reflect on your goals over the past year.

How are you doing?

1. Considering all of your objectives, what are you proud of, what have you accomplished, and what are you doing that works?

   Give yourself credit for every little thing you do that brings you a feeling or demonstration of success, even to the smallest degree, in any situation. Be specific, as in "When I was patient with Jack at the staff meeting, when I listened to him without interrupting even though I disagreed with him." Or, "I am proud of myself for making time for a family vacation while juggling client demands and book deadlines. Bringing the nanny to Hawaii allowed us to spend invaluable time with the kids—creating the kinds of memories that we will all cherish forever—and still manage hectic professional schedules."

2. What contributed to those successes? What caused those things to work? What has allowed you to do your best work?

How have you changed?

3. Think about yourself at the beginning of the year and the person you are today. How have you changed? What did you do that helped you improve? The activities may have occurred at work, home or in the community. Identifying the behavioral factors or improved mindsets that proved to be a positive catalyst. That will allow you to use them as tools in the future to replicate those successes.

Going beyond!

4. Now think beyond your given objectives. What achievements, accomplishments, or activities are you proud of?

Becoming even more effective.

5. To make yourself even more effective in the future, what do you want to continue to do, do more of, do better, or do differently?

   Of all the items listed and described above, which are the ones you are inspired to act on?

6. What support do you have to do the things you identified in #5 (money, time, training, etc.)? What resources do you need?

(1)Inspired by <u>Now, Discover Your Strengths</u> by Marcus Buckingham and Donald O. Clifton

Part II: What Can You Leverage?

Part II: What Can You Leverage?

The second section of the book focuses on the foundational question: "What can you leverage?" I am not using the word "leverage" to reflect its typical relationship to power or wielding power. Instead, it is being used to describe your unique asset base and the context within which your assets have the potential to flourish. In this section, we will create a personal narrative and do some self-reflection on the many dimensions of our lives, realizing that intersections are where the potential lies.

Jerome Offord is one of my dearest friends and among the people I most admire. We met when I was a senior in college and he was in his first year of graduate school. Jerome grew up on the South Side of Chicago, the oldest of three children raised by a single working mother, with the support of his grandparents and aunts. Jerome was a first-generation college student like me, who went to school because a village of people along his life's path believed in him and because he, despite the odds against him, had great belief in himself. While his mother worked multiple jobs Jerome helped raise his younger brother and sister and lent a hand at his grandparents' soul food restaurant. He developed a strong work ethic at a very young age. As a child, Jerome's aspiration was crystal clear: "I want to make my Mama proud."

When I met Jerome he had already tackled the major life hurdles of getting into college and completing his undergraduate education. Let me spell this out to clarify the magnitude of that accomplishment. Jerome was first generation, poor, black and a male from a tough neighborhood in a tough city — a male who benefited almost solely from female role models and had little access to people who could help him shape an identity as a black man. In addition, he had a relatively weak educational foundation. He has always been intelligent and willing to work hard, but "book smarts" weren't his gift nor were they emphasized by the adults in his adolescent life who were hustling day-in-and-day-out to put food on the table. As I said, getting a bachelor's degree and being admitted into graduate school was quite the impressive accomplishment at that point. But there's even more to Jerome.

Jerome went on to receive a master's degree in Student Affairs in Higher Education. Throughout his graduate school program he worked nearly full time, was actively involved in Alpha Phi Alpha Fraternity, Inc., did the research and completed the seemingly endless paperwork to successfully launch a not-for-profit organization focused on providing educational experiences to young people.

After completing this degree Jerome moved to Washington, D.C. and plowed in to his work. Though he had ambitions to be a university administrator and grow his not-for-profit, he understood that hard work is essential at the beginning of one's career in order to build skills that are based in reality and grow a reputation as a person who is able to follow through. Every step of the way, Jerome became masterful at networking. He talks to people in his easy, open way. He makes connections with people with whom he has a lot in common, and finds common ground with people who at first glance he shares little foundation for a relationship. People love his approachability and his "can do" attitude. Most of all, he always, always does what he says he's going to do—always.

I trailed Jerome to D.C. when I completed my master's degree. After a few years I was in the fortunate position of being able to hire someone to fill a position that I was leaving because of a promotion. Jerome immediately came to mind and he accepted the position, even agreeing to pursue a second master's degree in order to immerse himself in a new professional field.

Jerome blew me away. Walking into my previous position could have been intimidating for him. I was well-liked in that role by the professional community, and had experienced great success managing the program. Showing his political savvy, he didn't try to fill my shoes. Instead he came into the role, asked a lot of questions, listened attentively to the answers then focused on maintaining the inroads I had already made while breaking into new territory that uniquely capitalized on his strengths.

For example, he drew on the strong relationships he had within his fraternity to build a robust communication system. He used the administrative and organizational skills he developed in creating his not-for-profit to pursue grants — all of which were awarded. At the same time, he breezed through his second master's degree and then onto a PhD program, held national positions within Alpha Phi Alpha Fraternity, Inc. and is now a Dean at his alma mater, Lincoln University in Missouri, where he continues to give back to the community that nurtured him and that he (and I) still love. Jerome took a potentially tragic story about a poor black kid growing up in a single parent home and turned it into a triumphant narrative of perseverance. And this is a story that he shares every day as he walks the walk, still mindful to always do what he says he will do — always.

Chapter II

"Housewives"

Only Show the Glam and the Drama

Housewives Only Show the Glam and the Drama

Who raises "Housewives'" children? With the exception of seeing Kyle consoling a squirming curly-headed toddler during a pool party, their children always seem to be totally self-contained, if they're seen at all. They're dressed and fed, their hair combed. They don't require hours of their parents' time sitting at the dining room table laboring over homework and school projects.

And what about those houses and cars and wardrobes? Hell, even their closets are perfect! You and I both know that there are lots of pieces left out of the scenes we see, that the complicated, messy, unpretty realities are intentionally omitted from our view. For television, this approach makes sense to me, but I find that a lot of women (myself included) often try to live this way in real life.

We strive to create artificial facades that make everything look perfect. We hide and are even ashamed of what we feel is less than perfect, by our own and others' standards. But here's a reframing opportunity: consider redefining perfection to include the stuff that makes your life's stories rich and that deeply informs your identity.

Traditionally we have taken a uni-dimensional approach to identity. We tend to think of and describe a person as a woman, African American or other ethnicity, or a Gen-Xer, or a single mother. In contemporary discussions about identity we take a more multi-dimensional approach.

Because who I am provides special contexts for my journey, it is repeated perhaps too often but necessarily so. I am a 41-year-old biracial woman, first-generation college graduate who now has degrees in psychology, higher education and an MBA. I am an entrepreneur, a mother, a life partner. I have traveled around the world speaking on leadership and management.

As an introvert I have gone beyond my natural comfort zone to coach CEOs and consoled grieving parents. I take my kid to school in the morning and pick him up in the evening. He and I practice piano together in the morning and before bed. We sit at Starbucks and eat pumpkin bread while we discuss our day's events. We ride bicycles. We watch the sun set. I'm a multi-dimensional person and so are you. All of us have many aspects of ourselves that make us uniquely the people we are, and aspire to be. This chapter is about harnessing you—all of you.

I have spoken about multi-dimensionality for years and years before ever using the phrase. Multi-dimensionality is a simple and powerful concept because it acknowledges and provides access to the unique intersections of our lives' experiences, our talents and aspirations—to help achieve desired results. It's also important to realize that these characteristics may fluctuate over time, with some being more prominent at certain parts of your life than others.

I have experienced this shift in my own life. I'm the mother of a four-year old son. Until four years ago I didn't associate with being a mom; now it is clearly one of the most important aspects of my identity – a particularly important topic for women. Many of us struggle—sometimes without even consciously realizing it—with this issue. Identity, in fact, sits at the intersection of self-perception and perception by others.

We have been pummeled by cultural messages about women's roles and subsequent appropriate behaviors. Culture transmits information about "what it means to be a woman" via family, media, religious institutions and dogma, friends, school—it's everywhere. And what are those messages? What were they when you were growing up? What are the messages young women today are receiving? Real people have sometimes messy, multi-dimensional lives. With a little effort, you can pull those dimensions together to put yourself on your desired path.

Multi-Dimensional You

My father was one of 18 children in a family from a small Southern town, Marianna, Arkansas. He was a pre-teen when Emmitt Till, a 14-year-old black boy from Chicago who was visiting relatives in Mississippi, was accused of flirting with a white woman. For this crime, Till was abducted in the middle of the night from his great uncle's house and beaten, his eyes gouged out, shot in the head, then tied with barbed wire around his neck to the fan of a cotton gin and thrown in the river. His disfigured body was found a couple of days later.

Till's open-casket funeral was held with the permission of his family to bring the widest possible exposure to this atrocity. It set the South on fire and stunned the world. My Big Mama saw what was happening and sent two of her sons, those closest in age to Till, to the North where they ended up in a suburb northwest of Chicago, Illinois.

My father tells the story of his immediately being put into counseling. He didn't know how to interact with white people—having never had the experience and with his only psychological models being fear-filled. Through counseling and exposure to a well-to-do Jewish couple, my father turned his fear inside out and came to believe that the thing to fear was being considered black. So he set out to disassociate himself altogether from black folks, find and marry a white woman, and have him some light-brown babies.

My mother was one of ten siblings in a family from Illinois. Her parents are of German descent but they identified most closely with their religion, Jehovah's Witnesses. My mother grew up in a poor neighborhood that was heavily black and Puerto Rican. It's no wonder that throughout her adolescence she always longed for the brown skin and "big personalities" that she associated with black girls, and the black boys who liked them.

Of course, my mother and father were destined to meet. They were each filled with their own racial self-loathing and futile attempts to become more like the other. My parents had four children together before their relationship ended when I was eight. For the next 12 years I went back and forth between Illinois and Colorado, where my father had chosen to live. These were not merely visits. I actually moved, along with my mother, to different states and dwellings—sometimes up to seven times per year.

Iceberg Analogy of Culture

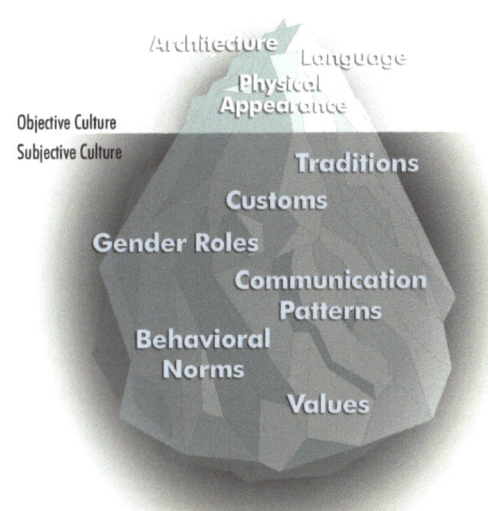

It was an interesting childhood. When in Illinois I was teased for being a "white girl." Our religion did not escape the wrath of other kids, either. Kids mocked me by shushing themselves and pretending to hide behind the curtains until the Jehovah's Witness went away. When I was in Colorado, in my father's all-white neighborhood near the foothills of the Rocky Mountains, I was seen as "rough around the edges" and exotic with my brown skin. Remember, this is before Halle and Tiger came on the scene. People who looked like me weren't in style yet.

Eventually — I'm still not sure exactly how this happened — of course, it must have been the Universe — I went to school at Colorado State University. College was overwhelming. I had a very poor educational foundation — remember, up to seven different schools per year from the time I was eight years old — and no learned study habits. I am also the eldest child and first-generation college student so didn't have access to anyone who understood University systems who I could turn to for guidance.

One of the things I found most difficult about school was the way that communication systems were set up. Most U.S. institutions, from schools to corporations, practice "low context" communication norms. Imagine culture—sociological and, in the case of a University, organizational—as analogous to an iceberg. An iceberg can be a huge, solid mass, with approximately 10 percent above the water line and the remaining 90 percent sitting under the waterline. Low context communication norms are the "under the waterline" parts of culture—the strongest, most deeply embedded portion that guides "how things *really* work around here." Some patterns consistent with low context communication are the expectation that information be delivered in a linear and succinct fashion, that feedback is given directly and close to the event, and that "you say what you mean and you mean what you say." In other words, there are no hidden messages. I call this the Clint Eastwood approach to communication. Think about your college essays, the last presentation you gave. PowerPoint. Succinct. Linear. Three bullet points contained in one slide—perfection! [1]

Now, I'm African American—from a cultural and ethnic identification point of view at least. Let me tell you about African Americans. We are expressive. Linear and succinct are a bit boring and unnatural for us. We are products of an African oral tradition and still love flair. After all, we invented "the dozens," a spirited exchange of insults about family members, particularly mothers. And rap was born when urban East Coast youth drew upon Caribbean "toasting" and homegrown "boasting" traditions in folk poems to create a new art form. We are storytellers.

I have a vivid memory of being five or six years old and asking my father a very direct question. A "Why is the sky blue?" kind of question that is typical of kids that age. My father looked me dead in the eye and said, "Did I ever tell you the story about the hawk and the buzzard?" He continued with a straight, even serious, face after a long pause: "They flew together for seven years and never exchanged a word between them. One day the hawk looks over to the buzzard and says, 'We've been flying kinda nice, haven't we?' And the buzzard looks back and says, 'You talk too damn, much.'" That was it. My Dad just stopped talking and walked away. What do you think, Reader? That about sums it up, right?

How would your five- or six-year-old kid respond to that kind of answer? To this day when I get in one of my states and I'm going on about something, my Daddy just looks at me and says, "Did I ever tell you the story about the hawk and the buzzard?" That's high-context communication. There's a lot of meaning outside and coded within the nonverbal interaction. And this kind of communication, in the form of storytelling, is typical in high-context cultures.

Now imagine my difficulty getting through college, a setting where linear and succinct communication is the expectation. Though I'm from the U.S. and English is my first language, I was in translation mode much of the time, constantly trying to figure out the rules for surviving in a low-context University environment without being adequately prepared.

About seven years ago I designed and led an "East/West-Leadership Institute and Cultural Exchange" between university administrators from some of the Ivy League schools here in the States and 30 of the most prominent universities in China. Chinese communication norms are much more high-context even than African American norms. From the moment we arrived in China until the moment we left, 10 days later, we were never without an escort. A Chinese ambassador was assigned to each of us and escorted us to every meal, meeting, and site-seeing opportunity. These ambassadors only left our sides at the end of each day after seeing to it that we were tucked away for the evening in our hotel rooms. Bright and early each morning our ambassadors were waiting at our hotel room doors to escort us to breakfast and through the next day's activities.

We ate every meal together. We went through elaborate toasting rituals every evening with dinner—the choreography of which was a complete mystery to any of our U.S. contingency. Only after three or four days did we come to understand, to ask and have it explained to us, that the toasting begins with the highest-ranking person in the room and then there is a known but unspoken order. We learned how to hold a glass when you're being toasted as the guest of honor, or as a lesser-ranking person who is touching glasses with a higher-ranking person and wants to show deference. We learned that "no" is never said outright. And most important, we learned about karaoke. I know this seems light-hearted but our trip was almost ruined because of our lack of cultural understanding and flexibility—diversity and inclusion (D&I) practitioners call it "cultural dexterity."

Think about it, my Ivy League administrators and their Clint Eastwood approach to communication. They weren't being smug; they were being "professional." Every evening just after the toasting began so did karaoke. Our Chinese counterparts would stand, one by one and sing full-length folk songs representing the regions from which they came. Some

of them were from farming communities, others from fishing villages. To a person, everyone sang...except us.

One evening on a chartered bus to the Laoshe Tea House I huddled with my American colleagues—all of whom were sitting together on the front of the bus, sunk down in their seats to avoid the wireless microphone that was being passed around for karaoke. "Come on folks, we can do this," I said. "We are cultural ambassadors." And then I went on to remind them that we are coming from a low-context environment into a high-context one—very high context. In high-context communication, the relationship precedes the business. "If we aren't able to make genuine personal connections that allow us to begin forming a trusting base, I'm afraid any of the other business goals we have in place are destined to fail. We have to show our good will as human beings." Later that evening, after dinner and with a few more mini-pep talks from me, we did karaoke—as a group—but we did it. We stood, went to the front of the room and sang our great American folk round—"Row, Row, Row Your Boat." We were brilliant, and got a hearty standing ovation. What could we do? A dean from Princeton looked at me and

Communication Patterns Across Cultures [1]

High Context
(e.g. Asian, Latino, African American)
- Much of meaning outside verbal communication
- Relationship is central
- Trust is foundation for relationship
- Social relationship strengthens professional relationship

Low Context
(e.g. German, United States)
- Verbal language conveys literal and full meaning
- Clear lines between personal and professional relationships
- Communication is direct and close to events

said, "We should do one more." That was the tipping point in our trip. To this day those business relationships continue to flourish.

This is how culture works, and why it's so important to develop cultural dexterity as part of your core identity. The norms that are going to help us manage relationships, manage global teams and negotiate business deals across cultures will be cultural norms. They may be difficult to know at a deep level, but the concepts can still be understood and navigated well.

Over the years, the Mosaic of Diversity Model has helped me illustrate the ways in which the dimensions of ones' self are interconnected. This illustration is also useful in depicting the many access points to the topic of identity. When I work with groups, I first talk through the mosaic.

The Mosaic of Diversity is a visual representation of the many categories that make up an individual. The inner circle is comprised of those characteristics that are less able to be changed or influenced by external conditions. For the most part, the inner circle represents dimensions that a person has little or no control over (though, Lord knows, I try to slow the hands of time). The dimensions in the outer circle also capture significant elements of an individual's identity. The Mosaic is meant to illustrate how: 1) we are all composed on many dimensions; 2) our dimensions are intertwined; and 3) there are many access points to the discussion and understanding of identity. Our identities are like tapestries, with interconnecting aspects that allow our unique and multidimensional identities to be called forward.

(1)Low- and high-context communication description is taken from the work of Edward T. Hall, one of the founding fathers of Intercultural Communication

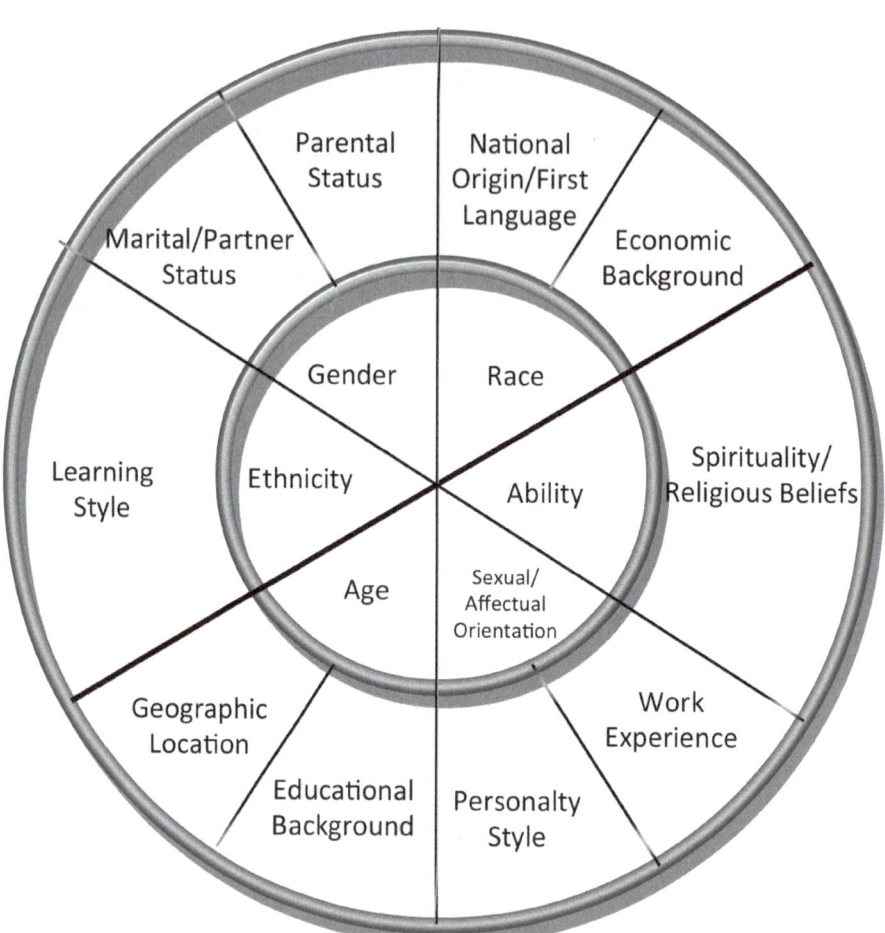

Mosaic of Diversity

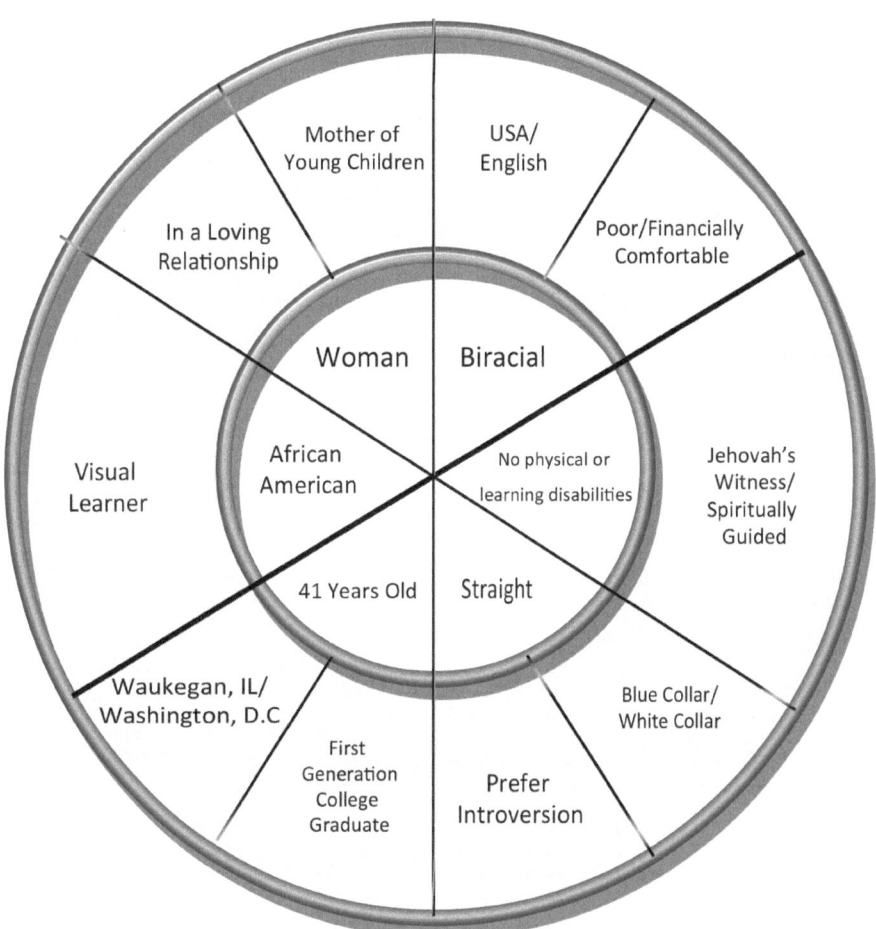

DeEtta's Mosaic

For clarification of the tool, I will share here how I personally describe the particular aspects of my own identity. I also share working definitions for the categories that I get questions about most often. In some cases I reference both "where I come from" related to a particular

category and "where I am now." This is because in some cases there is a vast difference between, for example, how I was raised or my life circumstances at a given point in time and my life circumstances and choices that reflect my current reality. I encourage you to do the same, as appropriate, when completing your own Mosaic. As you are doing this, consider how your upbringing or circumstances during childhood have shaped the values and beliefs that have led to your current reality.

Inner Circle Dimensions

    Gender: I am a woman who was raised primarily by a single mother of four daughters. My understanding of gender roles and the aspirations of women in U.S. society have been heavily influenced by the context within which I was raised. As an adult, I have spent many years grappling with my gender identity in a society that is going through significant growing pains in this regard.

    Race: I am biracial. My father is black and my mother is white. I do not elaborate more on my race in this section because it is covered in other areas of the book.

    Age: I am 41 yeas old and have been the youngest person in my professional roles most of my 20 year career. My youth, compared to others who have been colleagues over the years, has meant that I have spent a lot of time trying to prove myself to others—to earn credibility and respect.

    Sexual/Affectional Orientation: I am straight. I include "affectional" because I believe that one's orientation should also be defined by whom one is predisposed to fall in love with and that attraction is but a single component of a larger dynamic.

    Ethnicity: I identify ethnically as African American. My ethnicity is a reflection of the culture within which I was raised and see myself primarily belonging. I know that I am African American ethnically speaking because the lenses through which I see the world are African American. I know and am full participant in the communication short cuts and "under the waterline" norms that exist within the African American community.

    I spell this out because it is often the source of confusion, especially for white folks. I am regularly asked "Why do you identify as biracial in the racial category but clearly African American when it comes to ethnicity?" The answer goes back to identity—the combination of how I see myself and how others see me. My mother has often felt at a loss for a cultural identity because although she was raised in a primarily

African American community, as a Caucasian she was never fully accepted by that community as being "one of us."

In addition, her family, despite their long history in the U.S., did not have a primary ethnic identity and cultural practices that were handed down to her. You see, many European immigrants struggled to become part of the American "melting pot," shedding their ethnic names, speech and cultural practices.

Few realize that like African Americans, the cost of racism in the United States to many white folks has been a feeling of disconnection from their cultural roots. Though there are many people of color whose families have also been in the U.S. for many generations, our skin color has set us apart from the mainstream culture to a degree that has allowed, even facilitated, holding on to our unique cultural practices and identification.

Ability: I am fully able-bodied and have no diagnosed mental or emotional limitations. This category is tricky, particularly because it can and likely will change over the course of one's lifetime. First, as a society we are becoming much more aware of the range of disabilities and their impacts, including some of the unique gifts and strengths associated with conditions that we used to consider limiting. Second, for folks who do not currently have any disabilities, it is very likely that at some point in your life that reality might change.

My mother, for example, has a degenerative eye disease and is losing her eyesight. My entire life she has been an incredibly strong woman and capable provider. Now she struggles with reading even large font type, navigating her way around town, and enjoying simple pleasures like movies or time with her grandchildren. In addition, her life is filled with doctor visits and painful monthly procedures necessary to just slow the progression of the incurable disease. Though her experience saddens me, the reality of aging is that many of us will have some limitation that wasn't part of our earlier life experience and that significantly alters our level of ability.

Outer Circle Dimensions

National Origin/First Language: I was born in the U.S. and my first and only language spoken is English. For those of you who have an answer similar to mine for this category, imagine what it must be like for a person born in another country or whose first language is other than English to navigate living and working in the U.S. Think about what it must be like to constantly be in translation mode or to convey a thought as convincingly as your native English-speaking colleagues in a meeting. I have actually been called into organizations to provide coaching for managers who are critically judging their front-line employees' performance because of their accent.

Economic Background: Again, this is a one of the categories in which I reference the past and the present. Much of my childhood was spent with my single mother who was raising four children and working two to three part-time jobs at a time. From a very young age, I clearly remember her encouraging me to pursue a job as a city bus driver so that I could have benefits and a free bus pass anywhere in town.

My current reality is quite different. I live comfortably in an upscale bedroom community, my house is nestled against a golf course, and my partner and I are a two-person income-earning team. But it is important to share my upbringing here with you because it informs so much of who I am and the decisions I've made throughout my life's journey.

For example, I have also been fiercely independent and am sometimes borderline obsessive about tucking something away for a rainy day. I come from poverty and worked hard to dig myself out of it, but I understand that the breaks afforded me weren't handed out to everyone in my neighborhood.

I understand that it takes an incredible amount of work, a huge support system, and more than a few divine interventions to break the cycles that bind so many people into poverty over the course of generations. It is with understanding that I regularly talk to my privileged friends, colleagues and neighbors, reminding them and myself of the opportunity—the responsibility—to be an ally to those for whom the poet Langston Hughes reminded us, "life ain't been no crystal stair." [1]

Spirituality/Religious Beliefs: I grew up a Jehovah's Witness. My religious upbringing instilled in me personal values and added a strong structural framework to a childhood that was often lacking structure in other areas. The Witnesses that were part of my life at that time were loving, generous, devoted and unhypocritical—they walked the walk. I consider it a blessing to have grown up as part of this religious community.

My early introduction to a religion with incredibly high standards for membership and based on authentic daily involvement and investment has guided my expectations and choices about my current affiliation. I am no longer a practicing member of any religious community but view myself, like many, as spiritually guided. My life and the blessings afforded me are clear evidence of divine presence.

Work Experience: My career has been "white collar" from the beginning. My decisions about the type of work that I pursued, and the desire to have a career rather than a job, is a direct outgrowth of the messages I internalized watching my parents. From them I learned about work ethic. Also from them I learned that I want to have as much control as possible over the decisions governing my employment.

Personality Style: There are a lot of ways to think about personality style. For the purposes of the Mosaic, think about how you identify on the Introvert to Extrovert scale. Introversion and Extroversion come from the MBTI (Myers-Briggs Personality Type Indicator) and reflect the source of a person's energy. People who prefer extroversion get their energy from the external environment and often times talk in order to clarify what they're thinking. People who prefer introversion get their energy from an internal source and typically talk when there is space—between the extroverts talking and thinking out loud—in the conversation. I like to use the following analogies: "Introverts = Think. Talk. Think." "Extroverts = Talk. Think. Talk." Introversion and extroversion are not an either/or alternative; they are two ends of a continuum with most people scoring somewhere between the two points.

I am more introverted than extroverted. This means that I prefer to get energy from within myself. It does not mean that I am shy or uncomfortable in social settings. I enjoy a good party as much as the next person, and can easily become the life of a party—but I need a bit of "me time" beforehand. Professionally, I spend quite a lot of time on stage talking to groups—for an hour, eight hours at a time, or for three consecutive days. During presentations, I give my energy to the group. Energy meets energy, remember? So my bringing my best and fullest energy to speaking engagements encourages participants to do the same; to give back to me their energy. This give-and-take allows the interaction to be "energy filled," but leaves me exhausted at the end. As long as I have a bit of downtime afterwards to recharge, I'm fully capable of continuing into the evening with the receptions, dinners and the like.

Educational Background: As noted previously, I am a first-generation college graduate. It was very difficult for me to get to and through college which perhaps has made me appreciate the achievement even more than some who weren't as hungry as for it as I was. I am now a staunch supporter of formal and informal education and believe it to be one of the greatest gifts, and commitments, in a person's life.

Geographic Location: I grew up in many places, primarily a small ghetto area far to the north of Chicago blended with a middle-class, primarily white neighborhood in the suburbs of Denver. I have never identified either of those places as home. Instead, I consider Washington, D.C. home. It was the first place where I found a sense of community; the first place I felt safe and welcomed and truly able to be myself. I have a funny story, though, about geographic location.

About 10 years ago, before Hurricane Katrina, I was in New Orleans for a convention. In between meetings and torrential rainstorms, I took a walk through the Garden District. It was a sunny early afternoon and I strolled among the huge and historic homes with a peaceful half-smile on my face, soaking in the essence of this mystical community. At some point, I made eye contact with an elderly woman sitting on a large porch in a wicker chair with a drink —in my heart I'm sure it was a Mint Julip—next to her. As I approached I allowed my smile to broaden and said, "This neighborhood is beautiful. I love these porches." She looked back at me and with a gentle smile but firm voice said, "Dahling, these aren't porches. They're veraaandaas." Yes, of course they are—verandas, in The Garden District of New Orleans. Yes, of course.

Geographic location is one of those categories that so many of us identify with on a daily basis but we often overlook when thinking about its effect on our identities. Think about the mythical Lake Wobegon " where all the women are strong, all the men are good looking, and all the children are above average," and its real impact on the cultural norms of people in the state of Minnesota. Think about the cadence of speech associated with people from New York City versus Charlotte, North Carolina versus Los Angeles, California.

Learning Style: This category is about how you learn. I am primarily a visual learning. My son, I think, prefers kinesthetic learning (also known as tactile learning) —to learn about something by engaging in a physical activity like taking something apart and putting it back together. Visual and kinesthetic learners are the vast majority of humans, though traditional educational systems were built for audio learners—teacher lectures, students regurgitate, teacher lectures some more. In order to help myself digest and retain information, I often write it down so that I can see it visually and process it in a way that meets my personal needs.

Marital/Partner Status: I am in a loving relationship with a person I respect and admire, and unmarried. I have been married before, so my curiosity about it and anxiety to meet some societally-set expectation has subsided. I also get questions every day about our (Richard's and my) intentions to marry. Culture does that; it puts pressure on its members to conform to its norms.

Parental Status: I am the mother of a four-year-old son, Shiloh, and step-mother to RJ, Sarah and Mary. Sarah and Mary are adults, so my role with them is based more in mutual respect and love. RJ, however, is only eight, so I have a much more hands-on role in his care and development. Having Shiloh was such a deep dive for me. Most of my life I swore off parenthood, clinging to my independence and remembering much of the childhood that was sacrificed to help raise my younger sisters. But he has been my greatest gift in life – a little heart stealer who has pulled out of me a kind of love that can only be described as motherhood.

Before Shiloh was born I had been intensely and solely devoted to my career. I have always had an interesting social life but prided myself as being primarily a career-oriented woman. Since Shiloh's birth, my professional priorities now take second place in my life. As far as I'm concerned, the Earth and Sun and Moon all revolve around him. I still work, maybe even spending more actual hours working now than before. But my choices are predicated by the desire to be a strong woman role model, a fully capable provider, and an emotionally-balanced mother.

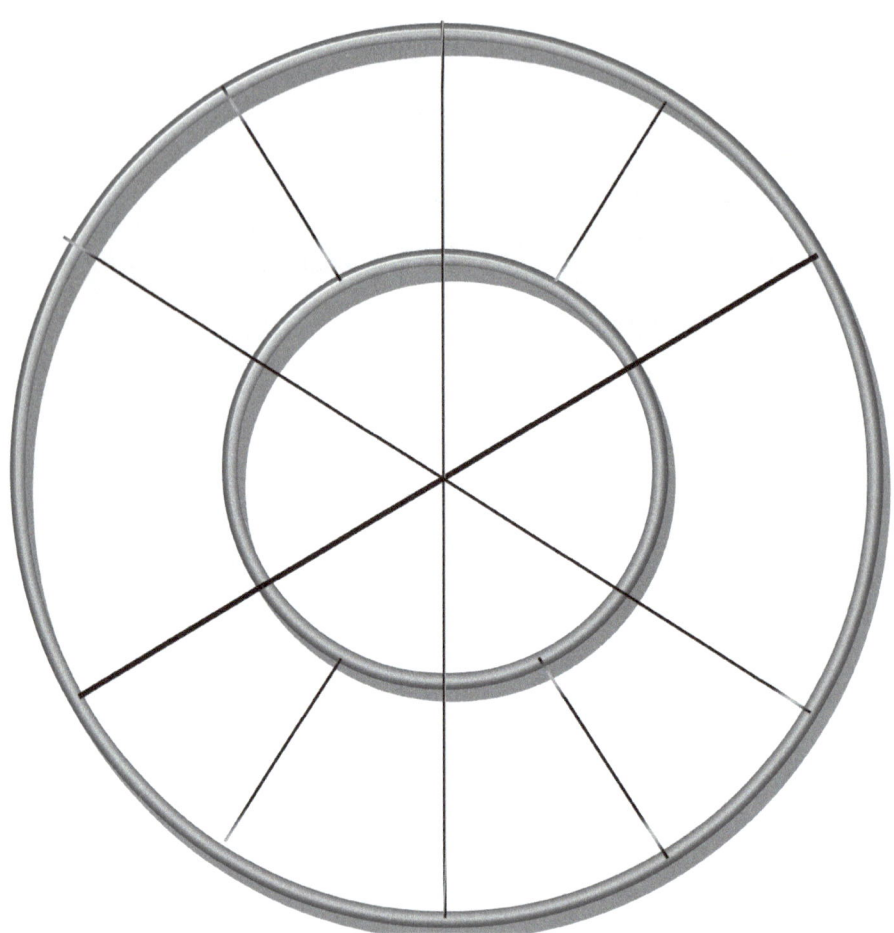

Your Mosaic of Diversity

Your Mosaic of Diversity

      The Mosaic of Diversity can be customized to your own experience and preferences. For example, my step-mother was adopted as an infant. She would likely add a category to her personal Mosaic that reflects being adopted and raised by adoptive, and loving, parents. When I have used this tool in workshop settings, some people have moved Spirituality/Religious Beliefs to the center of the model, to reflect the centrality of their faith to their identity. This model is meant to give you a framework for reflecting on and giving language to your own identity and experience. Don't let my categories, and solid lines between them, hinder your thinking. Customize it.

Exercise: Complete your own Mosaic of Diversity.

Exercise with a Mentor:

Share your Mosaic of Diversity with a friend or mentor. Share as much or as little as you feel comfortable with, but push yourself to disclose more or differently than you ever have with this particular person. Encourage the person to share something new about her/himself.

Have a discussion with your mentor describing what you learned about:

1. Yourself in the process of disclosing to another person. What areas of did you spend most time sharing? Why? What areas did you feel uncomfortable sharing? Why?

2. The other person. What did you learn that was unexpected/surprising to you? Why was this surprising? What new perspectives (access points) do you have about this person?

3. What will you take away from this exchange? What opportunities do you now have for future engagement with this person? What new ideas do you have for how you might engage others differently?

Finding Your Unique Voice

I believe we all have something special inside — skills, talents, perspectives. Some of us can easily put a finger on what is particularly special about us, while others are still trying to figure it out. That's okay. My only word of caution is for those who don't believe that you have anything special, or anything that distinguishes or sets you apart. That kind of thinking is deadly; it kills ambition, creativity, souls.

Maybe the real issue is that you are not sure of the context within which your specialness fits; the narrative within which your character has a role. For many years I have been inspired by Joseph Campbell's

The Hero's Journey and used it as a model for encouraging people to think about creating their own path.

In *The Hero's Journey*, the central character (you) are drifting through life when called to adventure. The "call" can be any major life event that triggers the need for new action and courage. Something as simple as reading this book could be a trigger for you. For others, it may going through a hardship such as a divorce, or the presence of a new opportunity like moving across country to begin college. Over the course of *The Hero's Journey*, the protagonist (you) go through various phases: "rejecting the call," "meeting a wise mentor," "tests, allies, and enemies."

Each phase is developmentally significant. The tests sometimes end in a setback, which requires re-grouping, picking of a wise mentor's brain, and re-focusing on vision. There are peaks and valleys, sometimes steeper valleys than higher peaks. The lessons are often painful. But here's the most important part: the protagonist (you) win. Because you stick with the journey, face the obstacles, draw upon the knowledge and support of others, you gain new knowledge, and overcome past obstacles that seemed insurmountable.

The final phases of *The Hero's Journey* are about metamorphosis—growth into a more mature, wiser, more confident version of your old self. I call this new-found confidence "swagger." And then you take that swagger and use it for the good of others. Nice story, huh? Look around, it's everywhere. It's the same motif that is the foundation for all great novels, great movies, great lives: from Oprah to Ghandi to Jesus to Dr. King to you.

I can think back on earlier points in my own life and easily draw connections to *The Hero's Journey*. My "call" happened in my late teens when I went to a predominantly white college in a small town in Colorado. I spent the first two years as an undergraduate grappling with my own racial identity. I spent a whole year being angry at white people for the ills of racism and the experiences of marginalization I had personally endured. Although anger is not an unusual phase in an identity development process, it's exhausting.

By the end of my sophomore year I took a more positive approach and began to seek out other outlets for self-expression. I was fortunate enough to meet my "wise mentor," Barb Kistler, a teacher who gave me language to make sense of my feelings. She listened through my anger, without judging or becoming defensive, though she herself was a white woman and could have justifiably reacted differently. She facilitated my growth.

Then, in my junior year I met and began a love affair with a white guy named Billy, who was in my anatomy class. He always sat in the front row wearing these sexy horn-rimmed glasses. He had great hair, a huge smile, and strutted like a brother when he walked. White-boy swag, big time. I was a biracial kid who grew up poor and underexposed to anything cultural. I knew "Good Times," "Soul Train," and enough about Malcolm X to wear a t-shirt sporting his image.

By contrast, Billy was from Denver, the son of a stockbroker and an elementary school teacher, both of whom encouraged their children to be citizens of the world. They were taught to give generously in the name of charity, and to nurture friendships with people of other races and social classes. Billy and I were inseparable. We made mini-adventures of everything. He got me a summer job with CoPERG, a not-for-profit environmental organization, canvassing middle-and upper-class neighborhoods. That was the first and only job from which I've ever been fired. I could talk to anyone but couldn't make "the ask"; I never raised a penny for the cause.

We took a road trip from Colorado to San Luis Obispo, put on wet suits and body surfed in the freezing ocean water. From there we continued north to sip on espresso and listen to poetry in the coffee shops of Haight- Ashbury, or walk barefoot across the UC Berkeley campus.

In the winter Billy and I would drive to the mountains and snowboard all day, then spend the evening listening to Ottmar Liebert play his amazing flamenco guitar in a quaint Aspen theater while drinking red beer. On the way down the mountain we listened to Ziggy Marley's "Lee and Molly": "white guy in love with black beauty..." I blossomed because Billy allowed me to be me. He was one of the first people, and definitely the first man, who ever *saw* me.

The next winter, I went with Billy to spend the holidays with my extended family and his extended family in Chicago's northern suburbs. I spent the first few days with my play-sister and got my hair braided. It looked great—long, thick black braids hanging down my back. Then, on Christmas Eve, I carefully followed directions to Billy's great aunt's house where I would spend the next couple of days with his family. His mother,

whom I adored and who adored me, opened the door to greet me when I arrived at the house and immediately burst into tears.

Billy's father ran to the door to find out what was going on and console her. Barely able to talk through the tears, she sobbed, "She made herself look so *black*!" My body and soul ached. It took several months for me to face either of Billy's parents again, and our relationship was never fully restored.

The following summer, Billy and I went to the Juneteenth celebration in Denver. Juneteenth is the commemoration of the ending of slavery, so while people of all backgrounds are encouraged to participate, the vast majority of attendees are African American. As we walked hand-in-hand celebrating the end of one of the most oppressive institutions in U.S. history, Billy was targeted by two angry African-American men who jumped him for being with a black woman.

Within minutes, a mob was attacking him. I lost visual contact with him for several minutes as random people pounded and kicked him. He lost a couple of front teeth that day, and my body and soul ached again. I was reminded, and have never forgotten, that oppression can come from any direction.

Sometimes when I felt that Billy didn't understand me I would say, "But I'm Black! You can't understand what the world looks like through my eyes!" Every time, he would give me the same response. "Actually, you are a quarter African American, a quarter Native American and half European American. Stop repressing the parts of yourself that don't fit your current victim mentality. Embrace your full self!" You know, Billy was right. His maturity was ahead of mine, and ahead of society. He understood multi-dimensionality far better than I, and his teaching it to me was a gift I will always treasure.

I share these stories with you because they are consistent with *The Hero's Journey*. Horrible things can happen along life's journey, even when they aren't deserved, and even when we are trying to do the right thing. Some of these painful experiences were life-changing for me, and created the cornerstones of my career. I have spent the past twenty years teaching people about diversity and inclusion, coming from a fuller appreciation of the power of inclusion than I would ever have possessed had it not been for Billy.

And my experiential knowledge of the concept of multi-dimensionality has become a personal strength, allowing me to dip in and out of various personal and professional realities without feeling guilty or as if I'm abandoning my true self. Unlike the protagonist of *The Hero's Journey,* I can't say that I have overcome all of my personal and professional obstacles. But I do know that I'm certainly on the path and committed to my own metamorphosis.

Don't let your painful experiences become a roadblock. You are resilient. And you have the opportunity to turn past or present painful experiences into guides for your future. Be deliberate in your development. Rather than merely looking around and claiming to be the product of a particular culture or set of circumstances, place yourself in the role of narrator telling the story of your own life. Begin at the beginning, wherever that is for you (the "beginning" is often tied to one's culture). Articulate the milestones that led to major growth, carry forward the narrative so that it lays the foundation for your desired future. Become a hero.

Your Hero's Journey Exercise

Change or Transition Goal

What are you seeking to change? What do you want to do that isn't present in your life now?

Past

List 3-4 elements or discontinuities in your past that may cause people to wonder why you would either want to do what you are thinking about or whether you are capable of doing what you want to do.

Present

List 3-4 elements of your present that tie into or help you explain why what you are thinking is a good next step for you.

What resources (wise mentors, flexible schedule) do you have available to you and how will/can you draw on them?

DeEtta Jones

Future

What obstacles are you going to have to overcome in order to accomplish your goal?

Make a few notes about how your past and present make sense in terms of your envisioned future.

Part III:

How Are You Positioned as an Influencer Now and in the Future?

How Are You Positioned as an Influencer Now and in the Future?

At the end of the day, your brand is all you have. It's the sum total of your efforts and impact on this planet. My friend and Olympic Gold Medalist April Holmes is a great example of a person who manages her brand exceptionally well. Let me start by saying that April is a remarkable person. In addition to being a world-class athlete, she is the kind of person who radiates positive energy from across the room.

I met April just over a year ago at Michael Jordan's celebrity golf tournament in Las Vegas. I was there because Richard and Michael are long-time friends. They both rose to athletic superstardom in Chicago, Richard as the SuperBowl XX MVP and Michael as he led the Bulls to National Championships three times in a row during the 90's. (An aside, Michael is the godfather of Richard's oldest daughter, Mary.)

April was in attendance as the first woman to represent the Jordan Brand, and among her peers as an elite athlete. We first met at an evening reception that makes the song "Bringing Sexy Back" seem like a children's tune. She walked in, in full swagger mode, with a stylish Jordan-brand sweat suit and sneakers inspired by her, and that are made especially to fit her prosthetic foot.

April is touted as the world's fastest female amputee. Prior to the accident that led to the loss of her left leg, she had been a leading sprinter at Norfolk State University. After college, she secured a good job at a communications company. Her true love was running, but she felt grateful that her track and field abilities paid for her to attend college. She was quoted in an interview as saying, "I would always ask God for a job in sports or entertainment where I could travel and meet different people." "Then, Voila! I got it. My only thing was I wasn't specific in my prayer. I never said, 'God can I have 10 toes, too?'" said April.

In 2001 a freak train accident left her without the lower part of her left leg. She laid in her hospital bed trying to imagine the implications for her life—her career, ability to pay hospital bills and manage her mortgage and car payments, relationship with then boyfriend, and love of running. To help her open up her mind to the realm of possibilities, one of the attending physicians gave her a magazine that highlighted the Paralympics.

Even before April was released from the hospital following her amputation surgery, she was determined to be the best at the Paralympics Games. And a little over two years after losing her leg, she broke three world records at the 2004 Athens Games. At the 2008 Paralympics, April was in the lead at the 200-meter final in Beijing when the spike on her prosthetic left leg got caught on the track, causing her to fall and hit the ground hard. Another runner stepped on April's face with a track spike. With blood pouring down her face, she picked herself up and completed the race.

"I have this thing about finishing whatever you start, so despite my condition I was going to cross the finish line,' April wrote. The same article goes on to say, "A few days later, despite that injury Holmes raced in the 100-meter final. Her leg and hips hurt so much she could barely continue training. She won the gold in the 100 with a time of 13.72 seconds, which is just three seconds slower than the Olympic record held by Florence Griffith-Joyner. Holmes would later discover she did it all with a labial tear in her left hip."

Wow! And all that was just prelude to the real reason I inserted April in this section of the book. I didn't know about her title or athletic accomplishments when I met her, yet I was compelled to meet and try to establish rapport with her. You see the most amazing thing about April, from my perspective, is her character, which radiates from her. She is at once confident and approachable, though she could have easily been inaccessible and arrogant.

Keepin' it classy—on Twitter, on Facebook, on YouTube, on Instagram, translates into business deals worth big bucks.

During a recent dinner conversation I told her about this book and about my concern with how women are either not proactively branding themselves, or doing so, but in ways that are less than flattering. April went on to recount for me an exchange that she had with a company executive during a sponsor negotiation session.

The sponsor told her that he reviewed every tweet that had ever come from her Twitter account, read every article that had ever been written about her, and watched every interview she had ever given. He then went on to compliment her about her public presentation—everything was not only squeaky clean, but it was filled with positive messages of encouragement to fellow athletes, praise for her sponsors, and overall classiness. Knowing enough to know that I can never understand what it's like to train at Olympian levels in every interaction with her she praises God and her mother for all that she has been able to accomplish. Think about it. Keepin' it classy—on Twitter, on Facebook, on YouTube, on Instagram, translates into business deals worth big bucks.

Recently I stumbled upon another article on April's career and amazing journey that started with this quote from her: "I believe I am my toughest opponent because I always expect greatness out of myself!" Yep, that's my friend. She raises the bar for me with every encounter. She expects greatness of herself, and it inspires me to reach for greatness too. That's the best kind of friend to have, isn't it? Someone who is better than you at something? Someone who draws out of you the potential that may be sitting dormant or that insecurity has obscured for far too long.

Chapter III

"Housewives"
Have Editors

"Housewives" Have Editors

Identity is a combination of who I believe I am and who I am believed to be by others. The latter is often referred to as "reputation," "image" or "brand." In casual conversation on this topic, many people I have spoken with believe that their identity is purely, or at least largely, self-informed. It's a compilation of nature and nurture and the wide range of experiences one has had to date.

I believe that's certainly a part of the equation, but the power of others' perceptions cannot be understated. For example, I have worked with many executives who describe themselves altogether differently than do their direct reports, or—with often more pronounced differences—people several levels below them on the organizational chart. As a consultant, I am often called into organizations specifically to deal with this gap in perception; or more importantly, the repercussions that occur within the organization because this gap exists.

The Center for Creative Leadership assessed executives' self-perception and those held by others. They found a 1: .321 correlation between how executives view their behavior and how others view the same behavior. This means that 66 percent of the time executives are out of sync with their followers about how their behaviors are being perceived.

What are the consequences of not having an accurate understanding of how you are perceived? For starters, the existence of a gap of this significance is a clear signal that you are not receiving honest feedback. It is not unusual for executives to lack authentic feedback. They are often in peerless situations where the imbalance of power makes it difficult for people to share honest, sometime critical, information about behaviors for fear of retribution. Remember "The Naked Emperor"? [1]

Even executives who invite feedback or have little or no history of retribution against employees suffer from ingrained organizational norms related to communicating with one's boss. Another consequence of not having ongoing feedback is that one becomes susceptible to overuse of those behaviors that led to one's current level of success. At face value, repeating the behaviors that have led to one's current level of success seems like an obviously sound strategy.

However, it does not take into account the specific conditions under which those behaviors worked well and acknowledge that those conditions have likely changed over time. I see examples of this most often in people moving from manager to administrator level or from administrator to chief executive level. The behaviors of a top-performing manager—attention to detail, deep technical knowledge, operational excellence—are not the same as those of a top-performing administrator—strategic focus, broad knowledge base, ability to make connections between seemingly disparate pieces of environmental data otherwise known as "pattern analysis."

Have you ever said something in the heat of the moment that you wished you could re-phrase, explain or take back altogether? Sure you have, just like the rest of the people in the world. When we are in a highly emotional state, particularly one where we are feeling fear, we automatically go into attack mode. It's the "fight" in the "fight, flight or freeze" response and it's absolutely normal for mammals.

Here's the problem, though, with the fight, flight or freeze mode—it's limiting. As discussed earlier, it describes the state we are in when our neurological resources are re-directed to self-preservation and away from higher human functions such as analytical thinking. (Go figure!). I have a sensory input (experience) that triggers fear (anxiety, or threat, or embarrassment). Immediately, cortisol is released from my brain and it travels into my system directly to my extremities. It provides my limbs the needed fuel to fight (as in, a bear) or run (flight). But my brain is totally depleted of the needed fuel to think.

So I dumb down, literally, and lose the needed capacity for problem solving or creative thinking. And the trickiest part is that cortisol release lasts for several hours. I cannot shake this anxious, high-strung feeling for HOURS, let alone fully access the most self-actualized part of myself.

So why mention this? Because no matter what my neurological wiring dictates, I am responsible for being aware of and managing my own emotions, and my associated behaviors. And this constitutes what may be considered the ability to self-edit and thereby avoid often far-reaching consequences of impulsive behavior. The negative perceptions that emerge from these short-lived but dangerous episodes may ultimately be damaging to the personal and professional brand that we have worked so hard to build over time.

Sadly, many people lack personal accountability, regularly blaming others for their behaviors and the perceptions held by others. Sound familiar? If this is or has been you, take a step back, make an intentional choice, and do better next time.

(1) Refers to "The Emperor's New Clothes," a short tale by Hans Christian Andersen

Chapter IV

"Housewives"
Have a Hair and Make-Up Crew

"Housewives" Have a Hair and Make-Up Crew

I have amazing parents and sisters, a life partner that the Universe delivered especially to me, irreplaceable and loving children, talented colleagues, and wonderful friends: Melissa who got me through the agonies of high school; Kevin, Michelle and Alicia who stood by me during some of the toughest of my identity development stages; Cher and Tony, Evelyn and Thomas, my son Shiloh's godparents; and the rest of my amazing D.C. crew who cherish and support me with generosity without limits; and my new friends in Illinois, who have embraced me and made me feel like part of the family.

We all have a team, or at least, we need one. Build your team with a deep bench. These groups of people, those who are closest to you and those with whom you may rarely communicate but with whom you maintain strong rapport, are invaluable. They are your mirrors. They see you in different lights, and differently than you see yourself. They are the people who help you create and manage your brand.

In addition to stacking your deck with friends, family and colleagues that will provide you with a strong base for ongoing feedback, think about more formal ways of getting feedback into your life in the service of your vision.

Tips for Gaining Personal Insight

Outlined below are a few suggestions for gaining more insight about yourself and how you are perceived by others.

1. For young professionals who want to get to the next level: Find a leadership coach.

Select a coach who matches where you are professionally and with whom you can communicate well. Make sure that the coach understands your needs. Do you need problem-solving support for issues like managing employees' performance? Or supporting your work-life integration needs? Do you need someone to facilitate the exploration of your next step and long-term career options? Or are you looking for someone to help you map your transition into an executive position? In any of these cases, an outside party whose job it is to help you think methodically through options and support you in the decision making process is an incredibly helpful resource.

2. **For seasoned professionals who want to sharpen your edge and build organizational capacity: Commit to ongoing formal and informal assessment.**

Successful people are reflective. I know, I know. There are plenty of examples of people who are not reflective, not at all in touch with themselves and how they are perceived by others, and yet are in positions of leadership. This is true. Yet there are just as many recent cases of people like this who have fallen from grace—losing their careers, their fortunes, their credibility. Think about poor Kim Zolciak who seemed to really believe she was the next pop music phenomenon. Portrayed in the recording studio and giving performances on stage, people weren't laughing with her, they were laughing at her. Even a moment's self-reflection would have led her to this conclusion.

And for the rest of us with ambition remember, the higher up you go in the formal leadership ranks, the more important it is to truly commit to self-betterment, making small adjustments along the way that will keep you from experiencing a major career setback. Today, 360 degree assessments are increasingly common for executive leaders' performance evaluation. With that said, I strongly discourage one's first exposure to a 360 degree assessment come through a performance review process. Rather, 360 degree assessments are most helpful as developmental tools, so seek out an opportunity through your boss or the Human Resources office to get this sort of feedback when you can use the input to guide your future behaviors.

Seek out voluntarily, too, an opportunity to participate in a 360 degree review as part of a leadership experience or a succession planning effort. You will use the same type of instrument so popularly used as a performance tool for senior leaders, but within the confines of a learning experience that allows you to receive the feedback, internalize it, and then work to make needed changes. This approach also means that you are taking control of your perception, and reinforces your reputation as a credible leader who is willing to walk the walk.

3. **For someone who is looking to develop a particular skill set: Get a coach or take a class. Do something structured that helps you keep your focus, allows you to have feedback on performance and progress, and holds you accountable for follow through.**

The most important thing I can say about feedback is this: embrace it. If "perception is reality" is indeed correct, it's worth the personal effort to seek feedback regularly and act on it. Relatively minor course-corrections in behavior keep the perception gap small and manageable—decreasing the probability of being blindsided. Feedback should be considered a 6 to 1 ratio. For every time you give someone corrective feedback, you should have six times provided that same person feedback about how her/his behaviors were helpful and should be repeated. The same is true for receiving feedback. Find out about the areas in which you are doing well. These are important for you to know. Here's another thing about feedback, if you don't want it and won't be influenced by it, don't ask for it.

Feedback is most effectively given and received if both parties understand the motivation behind the request and believe that information is being shared in the best interest of the soliciting party. As the recipient, I must believe that honest feedback is going to give me helpful insight that I would not otherwise have access to and that will help me make useful behavioral decisions, about repeating certain behaviors or making changes. If I am not willing to change my behavior, I should not ask for feedback. Inviting feedback creates an expectation on the part of the person giving the feedback. If that expectation isn't met, she/he will likely not be willing to honor future requests of the solicitor.

My second piece of advice related to soliciting feedback is to focus the invitation. It's difficult to know where to begin when asking for feedback. "Do you have anything you'd like to share with me?" "Are there things I'm doing about which you'd like to give me feedback?" These are not quite specific enough questions. While they are open-ended and invite commentary on any number of behaviors, it's more helpful to focus the inquiry.

It's also helpful to remember that it's difficult for people to give feedback about you, as a person. Particularly if a solid and positive relationship exists, people are hesitant to share criticisms about what may be perceived as one's personality or character. Instead, focus on behaviors and/or a situation that is bound by a focused period of time. "I'd like to hear your thoughts about what went well at today's Cabinet meeting and what might be done to encourage higher levels of contribution from everyone." "It seems to me that we're having some difficulty seeing eye-to-eye on how to proceed with the next phase of our plan. I think we share a vision of where we would ultimately like to go but would like to get your input about how we might approach this initiative differently, to get us on the same page."

4. For Everyone: Find a Mentor. Find Several Mentors.

Within a mentoring relationship, giving feedback needs to be couched as one element of a multi-faceted and constructive relationship. Let us explore mentoring relationships here.

The Gift of Mentors...and Dangers of Anti-Mentors
Definitions

Mentoring: A mutually agreed upon relationship between people who commit to pursue an intentional agenda that primarily focuses on the growth and development of the protégé.

Mentor: Someone who 1) has experience-based wisdom in a particular area and 2) actively invests in the development of another person.

Protégé: A person seeking growth in a particular area of her/his personal and/or professional life and is committed to learning from and with a person possessing experience-based wisdom.

Anti-Mentor: Someone who actively subjugates others and/or models undesirable behaviors.

"The Housewives": See Anti-Mentors.

I have been helping people develop leadership and management skills for nearly two decades. I have created and facilitated leadership and management programs for thousands of people around the world, and each of them includes segments on personal awareness and the importance of having mentoring relationships.

Mentoring is key for leadership development, for young people who are at the early stages of crafting their identity, for managers who are looking for models to help shape, articulate and execute against the backdrop of a vision, and for people who are more seasoned in their lives and careers and understand the significance of giving back as integrally connected to creating a legacy.

As for me, I was a first-generation college student who was sorely in need of guidance. My first two semesters of college were filled with missing classes, poor study habits, partying and the resulting 1.6 GPA. Without my looking for them, without even knowing what they were at that point in my life, mentors appeared for me. They were people on campus such as Barb Kistler who was the first person to listen to me and encourage me to be reflective.

She was followed by Dr. Albert Yates, President of Colorado State University, who created an assistantship in the President's Office for me so that I could earn money for tuition and housing while being closely monitored by responsible adults – an essential condition for me at that time. And Dr. Blanche Hughes, then Director of Black Student Services, who helped me find grants and encouraged me to connect with other African American students on campus, but in constructive and organized ways rather than at fraternity houses and tailgating parties.

Countless other people stepped into my life during my undergraduate and graduate years, all playing some critically important role in my early identity development process. For me, they were the difference-makers who opened up the world to me in ways that afforded me greater access to resources, helped me re-focus energy from destructive to constructive activities, and guided my intellectual and social development at a pivotal stage in my life.

Beyond this point, I continued to need and depend on mentors but for different purposes. I actively sought out people who could help me transition from a young adult to a young professional and emerging leader. The previous group of mentors had piqued my curiosity about the world and my place in it. They showed great faith in my potential.

This next group of mentors represented people who could help me get from potential to impact. Alma Vigo-Morales taught me about professionalism, poise, and how to use my unique cultural perspectives and style as assets—particularly as I was often, and have since been, one of the youngest and few people of color in a room full of decision-makers. Ann Azari, then Mayor of the City of Fort Collins, supported me, at only 25 years old, taking on the role of interim Director of the Human Rights Office. Jaia Barrett, Duane Webster and Kathryn Deiss took me under their wings as a new program officer at the Association of Research Libraries, grooming me in a new professional role and for an international stage. And Karin Trainer, Princeton University's first woman University Librarian, was the first university administrator to invite me to share my thoughts on the state of diversity and inclusion with the entire campus community.

Of course, there were many others who played important roles during this stage of my life too. My village was large and diverse. All of us have, or at least have the potential to have, positive folks in our lives who can support our development. If you take advantage of these personal resources, your life can be immeasurably enhanced. By the way, mentoring can be just as fulfilling for mentors as for protégés. Many years later I continue to have strong personal and professional relationships with most of the people previously mentioned. Often I am giving as much to them now as they have given me over the years—it's an ecosystem.

The final mentoring stage is related to legacy; it's where I am now and Richard is one of my primary mentors. He consistently encourages me to lean into my discomfort, to stretch, to do more. It's frustrating but stimulating – just what I need. And that is what mentors do: help you get just what you need just when you need it.

Mentoring Relationship Roles

In establishing and maintaining a solid mentoring relationship, certain conditions must be met. Both need to share enough to establish rapport, agree to level of confidentiality and expectations regarding communication style and frequency. Whether concentrated for a short period of time or one that will span for a longer duration, this relationship must include an explicit commitment to care for and respect each other.

Sometimes protégés approach a mentor with a specific "ask" in mind. For example, one request I typically hear from mid-level managers is, "I'd like a mentor who can teach me about budgeting." This desire is perfectly acceptable for a more junior person, and a helpful mentor may, in that instance, recommend a budgeting course or set aside time to walk through budgeting spreadsheets used by their company or in a particular department.

Coming from a mid-level manager, however, the request to learn more about budgeting might be considered differently. The mentor's role is to listen to what the protégé is saying but through the lenses of her/his experience. A helpful mentor may say in response to the aforementioned request, "Given your senior leadership aspirations, what I think would be more helpful for you is to learn about the budgeting and resource allocation process—the cycle, the politics, how to position yourself to get a seat at the decision-making table."

Mentoring Relationship Roles

Protégé	Mentor
Reflects on needs and defines the scope of the relationship	Creates learning experiences and exchanges that respond to protégés needs
Describes goals	Listens and uses personal experience and insight to appropriately challenge the scope of protégé's goals.
Reflects on needs	Matches personal experience and resource base with need needs of protégé.
Actively listens	Actively listens
Asks for feedback	Asks for feedback

I encourage you to find mentors that represent the strongest and most significant parts of yourself— those three to five core assets that most capture your essence. Mentors are people who can help you extend portions of yourself that are already strong. I'm a big proponent of building from a place of strength. It's the only way to get, in the words of author Jim Collins, from Good to Great. And it is far more helpful than focusing on weaknesses and expecting to develop those into strengths.

People are more motivated to practice diligently, repeatedly, perfectly those things that you are: 1) predisposed to do and 2) that you enjoy. So as you try to identify your strengths remember that they are built upon two characteristics, your talents plus your interests. Mentors should exude the characteristics that you already have and have the capacity to help you figure out how best to harness their potential.

Surround yourself with people who are positive, upbeat and who are where you want to be, doing the things that you want to do. Surround yourself with people who are making things happen. Put yourself into an environment that exposes you to peer-pressure to be better than you currently are—better, stronger, faster.

Be aware of the lure of idols versus mentors. Those "Housewives" you are watching on tv are not mentors nor should your sole purpose be to emulate their existence through your own life's journey.

Perhaps you want to be more fun and energetic. Surround yourself with people who display these qualities and but also the habits that ensure their outcomes are positive ones. They're not fun because they drink more or hang out at clubs more. They're fun because they find the positives in life and bring them forward. They're fun because they fully appreciate their families and spend time with them. They're fun because they have rich social lives that include personal relationships, philanthropy or some form of giving back, community engagement and careers that make them feel whole and give them feedback that is positively reinforcing.

They are vibrant because they have disciplined exercise habits and robust spiritual lives that keep them energized and whole. Find people who read as much as you wish you read, who have the kinds of quality relationships with their children that you wish you had, who exercise as much as you wish you would exercise, who are as productive as you wish you were. Surround yourself with people like this and you will be anchoring yourself to a positive and aspirational peer group.

One of the people who has long been core to my peer group is Dr. Kevin Rolle, a dear friend and a great example of a person who has experienced, and come through, difficult situations well. That's the most we can hope for, right? Difficult situations are part of all of our life scripts.

We all have highs and lows, and hopefully there are more highs than lows. Ideally, we are thankful for the highs and have strong support systems to get us through and remind us that the lows are only temporary. I believe that how one gets through the low points in our lives is a testament to our character and even dictates the degree to which we can attain those peak achievements for which most of us thirst.

Here's my goal and my challenge to you: get through tough times well. Pay attention to how you are thinking about the difficult situation and figure out how it can be managed with the personal integrity and grace that you want to bring to any situation during the best of times. It's tough, of course, to live up to this standard when going through an emotionally painful experience. But setting the standard when things are good allows you to lay the groundwork now—to be prepared when the inevitable moment is upon you.

Don't go looking for it, or wait in dread for its appearance. Just make a conscious choice when you are fully able to access the parts of your brain that are focused on your aspirational self. My friend Kevin did just this, for one of the most difficult situations any parent can imagine.

Kevin's youngest son was diagnosed with cancer when he was just 9 years old. Kevin, at the time, was a high-ranking university administrator with career ambitions of being a president. He and his son's mother were divorced and living in different states. Kevin made the necessary adjustments to his professional calendar in order to be fully present during his son's medical diagnosis and on-going treatments.

While all of this was on his plate, Kevin remained a close friend and emotional supporter for a dear friend who, too, was battling cancer; and for me during a difficult time in my life. I clearly remember one full year when Kevin called me every single day by 7:30 am to "check in on you" and "make sure you're doing alright." He set the bar high for me in terms of friendship. He demonstrated for me how to go through a difficult situation without becoming so overwhelmed with self-pity that you are no longer able to be supportive of others who need you. He showed me how to manage the challenging times in life well.

In addition to formal and informal mentors, I find myself doing simple things to surround my home – my personal space – with constructive energy. I don't watch much television. My travel schedule and busy life don't allow it. But when I am home, I like to have the television on in the kitchen, even if I'm not watching it. I often turn to the OWN network, hoping to catch Oprah's Master Class or even better, Super Soul Sundays. Think about it, a yelling match where eight adult people are threatening to sue one another or Deepak Chopra talking about the power of prayer. No matter what your religion or how much you enjoy popular culture, this is not an apples-to-apples choice. The inputs to which we expose ourselves—even in the name of entertainment—will and do affect us. Choose wisely.

As I look back over my mentoring relationships to identify the common threads, I would say that each of my great mentors has demonstrated similar qualities. They:

- Focused on my needs;
- Did not try to change me into her/him;

- Did not tell me what to do, but guided me through difficult decisions I had to make;
- Allowed me to fail, but helped me recover quickly and learn from it; and
- Let me shine.

When I talk to groups and ask them to share the qualities of great mentors they have had, their list is very similar to my own. Interestingly and without fail, in each of those instances people have also shared examples of how the desire to not be like a particular person has shaped them. These people are potential role models, friends or teachers or bosses, who are unkind to others and behave in ways that are unflattering. I don't mean unflattering in a "that dress makes you look fat" kind of way.

The unflattering behavior I am speaking of lacks consideration for consequences to others is unethical and is solely self-serving. This unflattering behavior consists of actions that do not feed a higher good, do not promote growth or kindness or inspire others to act but prompt others to defend or cower. Insert mental image: Sheree yanking on Kim's wig or Taylor's "catastrophic meltdown" at the Ojai Valley Inn.

The terms "mentors" and "anti-mentors" are not meant to imply that within a particular person there is either all goodness and light or selfishness and mayhem. We bring our humanity to all that we do, personally and professionally. Each of us has strong points and weaker ones. Mentors are not perfect people. And anti-mentors are not evil—they're just not necessarily people you want to model your life after or that you want to help you (or would likely be interested in helping you) find a path, or hone a skill.

Admittedly, we have all been grateful for little slips made by exemplary people; it helps us recognize that they are human too. There's a certain release on the internal pressure gauge that makes us feel less than adequate as compared to those high achievers. But there is no excuse for poor management practices that create toxic work environments or interpersonal relationships that tear down rather than build us up. Perhaps taking time to consider how anti-mentorship is influencing us, individually and collectively, we can act with more intentionality and make new choices that support our becoming the people we want to be—not the people whose behavior is plastered all over your television screen.

Think about your own life and experiences. How many mentors have shaped you and how have they helped you become the person you are today? How many anti-mentors have influenced you and what effect have they had on you? My plea with this little book is that you, Dear Reader, will make intentional choices about the influencers in your life.

We live in a world filled with stimuli. I would go so far as to say most of us are over-stimulated much of the time. We have televisions with hundreds of channels; phones with unlimited numbers of apps and upgrades; jobs that require constant email monitoring and immediate response; children's practices, recitals and play dates; aging parents to care for; houses to maintain; social media from Facebook and LinkedIn to Twitter and, oh yeah, in-person friendships to nurture, and on and on and on.

With this many inputs, it is important to make conscious choices about how you will feed your soul, your identity, your career and your relationships. "Coveting thy neighbor" is a symptom of proximity. The 'Housewives' are in your house; or at least in most of the houses of most of the people I know, and they are having an influence on you.

They are embedding small daily messages about how life can (and should?) look, about the definition of success and beauty, about the focus of one's attention. Just like little boys often grow up wanting to be football stars because they are surrounded by it on television at home and in their schools, the Housewives are consciously and subconsciously shaping our definition of the glamorous life—without showing the connection to hard work, seeming to care about the adverse impacts on their relationships on a generation of people also trying to navigate relationships, or to the long-term consequences of primarily self-serving behaviors.

Sometimes the desire to find a mentor and become more like them has led to our becoming overly dependent or emulative in a way that causes you to lose your authentic voice. This can be a major mistake in achieving your goals. Admiration should not lead to literally following in someone else's footsteps. Being a carbon copy of a peer or predecessor does not produce success; embracing your own uniqueness is what wins the day.

Instead of trying to follow another person's path, blaze your own trail based on your own skills, strengths and abilities. These are the qualities that will set you apart in the marketplace. Do not interpret this advice as diminishing the importance of mentors. They are essential and have a lifetime of lessons and experiences worth repeating and avoiding. Mentors can provide invaluable feedback and open doors to networks. However, it is up to you to seize these opportunities. What will make you memorable is your personal brand, not the fact that you were introduced by or were the guest of your mentor.

One of the first functions that I attended in the mid-1990's after joining my new D.C.-based company was a reception filled with executives during a leadership development program for emerging leaders. One of my mentors and then boss advised us before we entered the reception: "Leave the room having met at least ten new people. For each of the people you meet, your task is to say or do something that secures you in his/her memory within the first sixty seconds." This was a daunting order. A lot of people do not feel very comfortable in a reception setting in the first place, especially with people that you don't know, myself included.

My group was walking into a room of executives, people who held the positions to which they aspired, so having access to this group was very intimidating – especially with the pressure we felt to maximize the encounters. Being interesting on the fly isn't easy.

It takes work to hone one's memorable opening statement. It can be as simple as asking another person about themselves or knowing something about the person you're approaching. In the case of the reception, these were all emerging leaders who were going into a room with all known leaders. They were meeting people they knew about but didn't know personally.

Housewives' have this down cold—over-the-top jewelry, $1,200 shoes, a toy dog, or double D's pouring out of low-cut dresses. But what's appropriate for the impression you want to make, personally or in a business setting?

In a setting like the professional reception described above, do your research in advance. Make a short list of people you must meet before you leave the event and review their LinkedIn profiles or timeline on Facebook. Put effort into learning things that will provide you with icebreakers, such as a common interest.

It's great to strike up a conversation with people about themselves and what they do; it demonstrates an interest in the other person, knowledge of their work and industry. It also shows that you understand the importance of preparation; sets you apart as a person who takes seriously the opportunities given to you and are eager to be considered a colleague or new friend.

Here's one more point to remember, just knowing about another person isn't enough. Ladder climbers, star gazers and wanna-be's will all know something about the other person, the "Big Dog" in the room. You are not in those categories. You are bringing something to the table. Be ready and willing to share it. I don't mean boasting or handing out your resume. I mean put your shoulders back, walk into a room with your own inner-mojo intact, open a conversation beginning with a genuine interest in the other person(s), link to common ground, then—Whamo!—let your strength surface.

For those who are uncomfortable interacting on the fly, prepare! There's no substitute for preparation and practice; these will help you work out the stress in advance and have your key talking points at the front of your mind, allowing you to focus instead on conveying poise and attentiveness.

This is also an issue for me. I am not a natural networker or socializer. I like people, but I'm much more comfortable on a stage than in one-on-one conversations. When attending these types of events, I remember that when I go into a room my job is to meet people, connect with them, and do something that is impressionable. I think of that as my job whether I am at a reception at a university where I just did a speech or if am at a social event with Richard. You don't know who you're going to meet, when and what opportunities are going to come up, who's watching, or with who you are in the room. In fact, it was in a setting like this where Richard and I met.

I'm telling you all of this but it is still not easy for me, especially given my preference for introversion. Sometimes I have to dig down deep and find the energy to go into a reception setting and make an impression or to go into a workshop setting and make an impression. Sometimes you have to push yourself out of your comfort zone. Even when you're tired, contribute to the discussion when normally you would not ask a question because you're nervous. Put yourself in the state of mind where you see networking as valuable all of the time. Do not be intimidated by people who seem to know everyone present or naturally gravitate to others.

It is extremely important to recognize and acknowledge that we are always making an impression. I used to see events as having work and social boundaries and the two worlds did not interact. That approach was limiting and not realistic in today's 24/7 globally and socially networked world.

In fact, networking for me takes place with other moms and dads at the bus stop, at a Bears game, Foundation events and in the nail salon. Be always mindful of how you're dressed, project a good attitude, beware of gossip or association with gossips, and show genuine interest in others. Something you're not expecting and might want to take advantage of could very well be waiting for you on the other side of an unopened door.

Create Your Identity, Manage Your Brand

> **A Case Study - Beyoncė**

We all know Beyoncė as a world-class artist who is firmly established in the global entertainment pantheon. But she also provides a consummate example of how one creates and manages an identity and brand of that magnitude. While her talent and drive are well known, she too faced a major challenge as a performer — natural shyness.

Even before establishing her post- Destiny's Child persona as a solo artist, Beyoncė developed a brilliant approach to overcoming her shyness. She created an alter-ego, "Sasha Fierce," who had all of the boldness, fearlessness and desired attributes of a mega-successful star. When preparing for a performance, the pressure was off Beyoncė to try to project the confidence that belied her shy inner child's tendency to hold back.

Remember, that she was doing what she had dreamed of doing all her life. Home videos show her as a very young girl expressing her vision of a career as an entertainer of the magnitude she has now attained. But the trick to defeating her shyness was to let "Sasha Fierce" take over and allow Beyoncė to go beyond her comfort zone to sing, dance and become the performer whose global success has been validated by the highest industry awards and breaking attendance records around the world.

But what separates Beyoncė from so many of her peers in the entertainment world is that she has carefully crafted her own brand as a class act driven by the pursuit of excellence in every aspect of her career. Like Michael Jackson, she oversees practically every detail — from concept to choreography, costuming and production.

But unlike Michael, she protects her brand by mastering the art of rising above the vicious attacks that all too often accompany superstardom — the relentless rumor mill that leaves no aspect of an entertainer's public or private life immune to speculation and fabrication. The birth of her first child was accompanied by a barrage of reports denying her pregnancy and use of a birth surrogate for her daughter Blue Ivy.

She ignored them all and controlled access to publicity surrounding her family.

Most recently, Beyoncé faced a media assault regarding charges of her lip synching her performance of the national anthem at President Obama's second inauguration. An ardent supporter of the President, she was thrilled to have been chosen for this honor and was surely rattled by the criticism of what had been a high point of her life. However, her handling of the incident was a pitch-perfect example of brand management. She chose to remain silent and headed for New Orleans to rehearse for her Super Bowl halftime show.

At a Super Bowl press conference to preview her show, Beyoncé answered her critics in classic — and supremely classy — style. The superstar began by making an unusual request of reporters: "Would you guys mind standing?" And then she proceeded to sing the National Anthem — live, unaccompanied, and in great voice. "Any questions?" she asked.

She later explained — for those who were still interested in what had now become a moot question — that she had not had an opportunity to rehearse with the Marine Band and do a sound check. So as a perfectionist — and 'fierce' protector of her brand — she opted to sing to her own track to insure a flawless performance for the President. And the country.

Perception Counts

On a personal level, my hope is that "keep it classy" becomes a little mantra that catches on with the same popularity as the 'Housewives' and the host of similarly themed reality shows. "Keep it classy" comes from one of my BFF's, Evelyn. She is the epitome of class—shoulders back, smile on her face, generous with compliments, genuinely happy for others' good fortune without the slightest hint of envy, able to care and listen without casting harsh judgments, and showers her family, friends and clients with the care and consideration they need.

Evelyn is gorgeous, married to a former NFL player, has a successful law practice, comes from an influential L.A. family. She could have chosen to define "class" differently, to focus more on material acquisitions or physical appearance or social status. But she didn't, and her classiness regularly influences me and others within our friendship circle.

A high standard has been set for all of us. It doesn't matter how pretty you are, or how skinny or voluptuous; how much money you have or had or pretend to have; what kind of car you drive or your man drives or your ex-man drives; who your baby daddy is or with whom you've slept. They are, in fact, only indicators of how low some of us allow the bar of individual worth to be lowered.

For those of you who are professionals, this applies to you as well. It applies to the value you place on your corner office and Chanel handbags and VP titles and country club memberships. It applies to the context of you as a friend, a spouse or girlfriend or booty call, a mom, a PTO chair, a manager or C-Suite executive. What really matters is less about the external stimuli—I call it "white noise"—that surround us and more about your connecting with your inner you and harnessing it.

My "keep it classy" mantra is for all of us who sometimes forget that our identity is shaped with every choice we make, every word we utter. Whether we're choosing to act or not act, we are still making a choice. Even our thoughts are choices—we choose to focus our mental and emotional energy on certain things over others. For all of us, let's make conscious choices about what we don't want to be, and more importantly focus on what we do want to become.

Here's my pitch—and I encourage you to include my definition of classy as your intentional brand—think of your life as a story to be displayed on a television show. You are one of several cast members, each requiring a clear identity that contributes to the overall theme of the show. Ask yourself, "Who am I relative to the other members of the cast? Am I the Protagonist? Hero? Victim? Underdog?

Mary Catherine Bateson, a cultural anthropologist, encourages the creation of a personal narrative. Psychologists call it self-authoring. Pretty powerful stuff, huh? You decide the story line. You position yourself in the role that is most desirable for you and others. Writing the story forces you to explore the needs and motivations of others; to develop the characters and your relationship to them—your colleagues, boss, clients, children, spouse or partner and friends.

This desire to understand what motivates others is a key to fully fleshing out your character's role and behaviors in enacting the story. It is also the essence of building a strong personal identity—understanding the needs and motives of others is one of the most effective ways to create a credible brand, a brand powerful enough to positively influence others.

When you consider your brand, think honestly about what others see. Remember, people only know what you tell them. The rest of what is assumed about us is just that – an assumption often based on speculation or guessing. Think about what you want to convey to other people, even without having to say it directly.

For me, for example, I have been told that I appear to be aloof. My response is that I am actually: 1) typically rushing to get from one place to the next; 2) often focusing on my own thoughts rather than on the environment around me; and 3) slightly uncomfortable in one-on-one interactions. The result is that I sometimes miss seeing people who pass me by or spending enough time engaged in authentic interaction to convey my care for the other person. Or I look too busy to be interrupted and so people hesitate to disturb me.

Although I am busy, I would much prefer to be interrupted than perceived as being aloof. It's simply not consistent with the view I have of myself or want others to have of me. So what I do is smile often—even as a million little thoughts prance around in my head. I remind myself that I am always on camera, metaphorically speaking, and that I am responsible for checking my own make-up.

A couple of things to remember about managing your brand:

1. Let go of the guilt. Not being "on" 100% of the time is okay. Sometimes people won't perceive you the way you want to be perceived. But give it your best shot anyway and know that your effort was honorable.
2. Don't be a jerk. Treat people well.
3. Don't gossip and avoid the company of gossips. It's unattractive in any light.
4. Share personal information in moderation. Know that some people will always find fault in you. Don't help them.
5. Stand for something but don't be inflexible. The moment you stop listening is the moment you lose some ability to influence.
6. F*@! what other people say. Be authentic and true to yourself.
7. Know when to keep doors open, and know when to close them.
8. Stay above the fray. When you have the choice, always chose the high road.
9. Be credible. Do what you say you will do.
10. Beware of overusing your strengths. In high doses, they can become flaws.
11. Choose happiness. Begin acting in accordance immediately.

Setting a Positive Tone

I am a huge fan of research on the impact positive emotions. Positive affect has been shown to lead to greater creativity, flexible thinking, as well as increased negotiation and problem-solving skills. People experiencing positive versus negative affect were found to be more ingenious and innovative when solving problems. Research measuring positive affect among medical personnel show that those students high in positive affect were more efficient, less confused, and more thorough in patient diagnosis than other medical students. Isn't this what we want for ourselves all the time—the ability to be high functioning and happy?

The tricky thing about positive development is that understanding it isn't enough simply to reap its rewards. We have to internalize it into our belief system then behave in a manner consistent with those beliefs. Most important, we have to model these behaviors as part of our regular routine, with everyone we interact with, and even under pressure. It has to become part of the fabric of who are as human beings. If a total makeover is a bit too much to ask, start with these things:

- Capitalize on positive events daily.
- Work toward a positive to negative interaction ratio of 6:1.
- Use Appreciative Inquiry techniques. (See: "Re-Igniting your Passion: Exercise")
- Enhance Emotional Intelligence, beginning with your own. Emotional Intelligence is "the capacity for recognizing our own feelings and those of others, for motivating ourselves, for managing emotions well in ourselves and in our relationships." (Daniel Goleman)
- Give feedback that acknowledges the role of positive emotions in daily work.
- Lead in a manner that is consistent with your values.
- Model positive behaviors (self-efficacy, hope, optimism, moral efficacy, resilience).
- Ask for feedback on the extent to which your behavior is consistent with your values and the quality of your modeling behavior.

A final point about positivity: practice it now. Don't wait until the proverbial shit hits the fan to try to recall some tip for managing through crisis. In times of crisis, people resort to doing whatever it is that they have practiced most up to that point. So if you've been treating people like a jerk or indifferently until now, when times are tough you will probably continue to do just that. And it won't help you.

Instead, think deliberately—now—about how you want to be perceived and the impact you want to have on people. Begin putting into practice actions that will help you make strides in that direction. Then, when the shit does hit the fan – and trust me, it will – your amygdala is less apt to be hijacked by fear because you have embedded thoughtful responses into your repertoire. You'll be able to access more easily the more helpful behaviors when you need then, rather than stuck in fight, flight or freeze mode.

Further, because you have been practicing behaviors that are positively impacting others and their perception of you, you will have built rapport for yourself. Even if you make a mistake here and there, the good rapport that you have built might buy you a "pass." I like to say, "We judge others based on their behaviors but we judge ourselves based on our intentions." Making your good intentions known early on and often allow others to be less critical, as we are with ourselves, in times of crisis or when mistakes are made.

Behavior / Impact Analysis

The Behavior/Impact Analysis is a practical tool for reflecting on your behavior and its impact. This is a tool that you can use for on your own or with a mentor. It can be applied to behaviors in any context—work, school, or interpersonal relationships.

Exercise: Reflect on a particular behavior that you exhibited. Describe it in the left column. Do not attribute motives or intentions here. Try to just describe the behavior as another person would see and judge it. After you have made some notes about the behavior, describe the implications of the behavior in the next three columns.

It is important to understand the benefits and costs, to your personal brand, of certain behaviors. Once you have completed the reflective exercise, think about steps that you should take to either a) repeat or extend a behavior that you believe is having a positive effect on your

brand or b) change or recover from a behavior that you believe is having a negative effect on your brand. I also encourage you to go one step further—to seek out additional input on reflections. This could come from a mentor or a friend, or even better, from the person or group who was involved in the initial behavior described in the left column.

A Word on Trust

Credibility is one of the most important qualities that people want in a leader. It is established by demonstrating your willingness to work hard, maintaining composure even during difficult situations, using logic and values to drive decision making, and all the other positive qualities that elicit respect and confidence.

It is also about the people. The most credible and successful people I know are genuinely interested in the lives and well-being of those around them, as well as how they are being impacted. Trust grows out of credibility. Once we have established a relationship that allows you to see me as a credible person, you have a mental model of me that is your touchstone. It also allows you to give me the benefit of the doubt when you see me behave in a way that seems out of character rather than judge quickly or harshly.

I am going to end this section by encouraging you, Dear Reader, to think about what you do on a daily basis that helps others to trust you—your intentions, your past and future choices. I used the word "do" in the previous sentence because like credibility, trust should be rooted in behavior, not just intentions.

One of my favorite sayings is: "You judge yourself based on your intentions. You judge others based on their actions." Again, what do you do to instill a sense of trust in you as a person? As a leader? What more can you do to help build and nurture trust? What can you do to repair trust that's been lost? Do it.

Behavior/Impact Analysis Tool

My behavior	My behavior's impact on the relationship	My behavior's impact on how I am perceived by others	My behavior's implication on my vision

Chapter V

Foolishness = Rewards *Only for* *"Housewives"*

Foolishness = Rewards *Only for "Housewives"*

We all make mistakes. Fall down. Get up. Dust yourself off. Move on—in the direction of your vision. Don't go back to where that last mistake led you. That's the difficult part, isn't it? Not repeating mistakes. Remember this: making the same mistakes over and over is foolish.

If you have read this far then I believe you actually care about how you present yourself to the world, and "foolish" is not an option. If you stay focused on aspiration and practice principles outlined in this book, you will be off to a great start on your life's journey. But here's the other thing, don't agonize over the mistakes—even stupid ones, even repeats. Give yourself permission to re-start. Patterns can be broken. They take gumption, and effort, and focus, and discipline. All of which are available to you. Make it happen.

Course Corrections

My BFF AP (yes, another BFF) and I met when I was 17 years old and a first-year college student. Our free-spirit personalities and shared biracial identities became bonding points for us. Through the years we supported each other through dozens of high and low points in our lives. One of the points along AP's journey was when she decided to leave her marriage and begin her life again, re-entering the workforce and as a single mother.

At the time when AP met her future husband, she was All But Dissertation (ABD) toward her PhD in Higher Education Administration. She had a successful career as a university administrator at a prestigious institution in the Midwest. Her future husband was also building a successful career and one that demanded a lot of hosting and attendance at social engagements.

He was drawn to AP's larger-than-life personality and ability to effortlessly charm anyone whom she met. After they married, they agreed that AP would put her career aside, help him grow his business and care for their infant daughter.

AP and her husband enjoyed a plush upper-middle-class life in one of the most prestigious areas in their home state. Their lifestyle included a custom-built mini-mansion, high-end vehicles, and hosting and attending lavish parties. AP had arrived!

I can say honestly that there were a couple of years where I just felt a twinge of envy about AP's good fortune. I worked hard. I put myself through school. I tried to date the right guys. And still I was on the hamster wheel. But then AP did something that knocked me back to reality, and humbled me immensely. She left her husband. She applied for and secured a job across country, with an annual salary similar to her husband's monthly income and off she went in search of a happier life.

Why did she leave? She left because the cost of staying, to her and to her daughter and over time, was higher than the pain of leaving then. As Anthony Robbins, the peak performance expert always says, "People change because of inspiration or desperation." R Kelly even has a song about it, "When a Woman's Fed Up." I call it *hitting rock bottom*.

Surprisingly, what I hadn't heard her say during all those years that she was married and living that fantasy life was that she wasn't happy. I hadn't heard her, or taken seriously, when she talked about the unbearable struggles and obstacles in her marriage. I was too focused on what I thought were the glamorous parts of her life to truly understand, or at least attempt to understand, her feelings. But feelings well up, and hers led her to an inevitable conclusion.

I asked her, shortly after she left, if she regretted any of it. "It was difficult to leave the financial security and my friends, and to start over with my career. Having my daughter not live with her father breaks my heart. But leaving was for the best. No one was happy and we all deserved the opportunity to live the lives that will be most fulfilling for us. Now [my husband] and I are able to communicate more effectively than ever and to co-parent our daughter. I just needed to get on the right course."

Two years later I decided to leave my own marriage. It was one of the most difficult choices of my life, and an agonizingly painful experience. AP saw it coming from day one. She patiently listened without judging and then gently told me, "You tried but you are past the point of return. Don't think of this as a failure, but a major course correction. Now go get yourself on the right path."

Sometimes we desperately need to make a change – a scary, scary change. Feelings of guilt, insecurity, uncertainty, doubt, shame and fear overwhelm us. For me, I was paralyzed by guilt. I felt guilty that I

married a good guy and couldn't "make our relationship work." I felt guilty that we couldn't have children together, knowing how important it was to him. I felt guilty that I was being selfish rather than thinking about all of the people hurt by a divorce. I felt ashamed to tell my family and friends that my perfect world wasn't so perfect after all. I was afraid of what my family, colleagues and clients would think, perhaps that I was flippant or indecisive or unable to make a commitment.

I tossed and turned at night, knowing that I was in the wrong place but not sure where the right place was for me. I didn't want to pull my young son away from a nice home and loving caregivers for an unknown destination. What would I do if I got sick? My husband was the one with health insurance. Where would we live? Could I afford all of my bills on my own? How would I deliver uninterrupted service to my clients in the absence of even a stable home base with an internet connection? Who would help me care for my son, knowing that my work requires me to travel? For more than a year I let these questions nibble away at my spirit. Then one day I felt desperate. I knew I had to leave right then.

> *"Focus on the goal, not the hits you're going to take along the way."*
>
> *- Richard Dent*

As Richard told me shortly after my leaving that situation but still reeling with anxiety from it, and drawing on his own experience on the football field, "Focus on the goal, not on the hits you're going to take along the way."

Of course, he was right; I took a lot of hits. But I am also now in a much better place for me. As I have said to friends and clients, in hindsight, I am now focused in the right direction. Before I was just increasing my effort and not realizing that I was facing the wrong direction. So all effort was futile.

Hitting rock bottom forced me to make a choice, to stand up and turn myself around so that I was facing the correct direction for me. Now, every step that I take still requires energy, but it's creative energy. It's the energy needed to get from current reality to vision, and it feels amazing.[1]

DeEtta Jones

Influence

My friend Evelyn is my "go to" person for guidance about how better to position myself within my relationship with Richard. That may seem silly, but all women have a "girl" we turn to for some rant therapy. Whenever the inevitable butting of heads that happens in intimate relationships lasts beyond the limits of my appetite for anguish, I call Evelyn to vent. (I have never mentioned this to Richard, but I guess the secret's out now.)

Evelyn is a great listener, partly a personality trait and partly her training as an attorney. She allows me to express my thoughts fully, even the ranting and raving. She keeps me on topic, allowing for minor tangents but knowing when to gently direct me back to the main point. She then helps me focus on the real "meat" of my argument. Once we've figured out what I'm really upset about (yes, it takes her skillful facilitation to get to this obvious beginning point) she starts questioning me about what I have done to let the situation get to this point. Here's a snippet of a recent conversation already in progress.

Evelyn: "What did you say to him when he did that?"

Me: "Nothing. I didn't need to say anything. He knew what he did was ridiculous!"

Evelyn: "No, he didn't. You have to describe how you are feeling to him right then and there. Then you have to tell him what you expect."

Me: "He is a grown ass man! He knows that asking me to get his dry cleaning when I'm sick in bed is inappropriate."

Evelyn: "Did you get his dry cleaning?"

Me: "Yes."

Evelyn: "Why?"

Me: "Because I figured he must really need it if he asked me while I'm laying sick in bed to get it for him."

Evelyn: "You should have said, 'No, I will not get your dry cleaning. I am sick in bed and not running errands in this condition. You'll have to get your own dry cleaning or wait until I've recovered.' As a matter of fact, you should have followed that statement with, 'And I would appreciate it if you dote on me a bit until I'm feeling better, give me extra help with the kids and let me rest as much as possible.'"

Me: "Evelyn, dare I repeat myself but he is a grown man. He should know this without me having to say it."

Evelyn, *The Insightful One:* "He doesn't know it. And he certainly won't learn it unless you clearly deliver the message and make sure that your actions are consistent with your message. It's your fault that he asks you to get his dry cleaning when you're sick because you actually do it. Set your standards high, tell them to him, and stick to them. Praise him when he behaves consistently with those standards. Revisit, directly and an in a timely manner, when those standards are being compromised."

Me: "Yes, Evelyn. And goodbye. I have to go get my talking points together now."

What was I lacking in this story? If you said technique, you nailed it. I had a problem that needed to be solved but didn't have a technique for getting what I wanted out of the situation. But there was something else missing too, or actually too present and clouding my ability to be effective—my frustrated emotions. Instead of dealing with the issue, I let my emotions spin out of control, limiting my options to employ tactful, diplomatic techniques.

Stuart Diamond, Harvard Business School professor and author of *Getting More: How to Negotiate to Achieve Your Goals in the Real World*, describes skillful negotiation as less than 20 percent about the substance of the issue, just over 30 percent about the process, and about 50 percent about the people. The people portion of the equation takes into account things such as likeability, the extent to which there is an emotional connection between the parties, credibility, the amount of respect, rapport and trust that exists. Reflecting on this a bit more, emotional connection is twice as important in your ability to be influential as substance (being right) and process (technique). So here's the million-dollar question for you: To what extent are you able to manage your emotions so that they 1) don't get in the way of your getting what you want, and 2) allow you to be as influential as possible?

Developing Your Influence Skills

Understanding the techniques you prefer to use to influence others will help you get the results you want and need, in daily interactions as well as in the service of your vision. The nine influence strategies described below come from a personal assessment tool developed by the Hay Group. These strategies are based on research conducted beginning in the late 1950's and were then built upon and combined with 15 years of applied research to identify the most common and effective strategies for influencing others.

These are the specific behaviors that help us influence most successfully. It is important to emphasize that all of these strategies can be effective in the appropriate context. They can also become ineffective when used inappropriately.

Develop Your Skill: Strategies Used by Influential People

1. **Empowerment:** valuing others by giving recognition and involving them in the decision-making process.
2. **Interpersonal Awareness**: positioning your ideas to address the concerns of others.
3. **Bargaining:** exchanging mutually desirable favors or resources.
4. **Relationship Building:** establishing and maintaining rapport with a broad range of people knowing that you might call upon them for support in the future.
5. **Organizational Awareness:** identifying the key influencers in your group or organization and getting their support so that they can, in turn, help to promote your agenda.
6. **Common Vision**: connecting your individual or group goals to higher principles such as fairness.
7. **Impact** Management: presenting ideas in interesting, memorable, or dramatic ways to establish an emotional connection with your message. For example, think about the last time you heard a presenter at a fundraiser open with a great story about how someone's life was changed because of a generous act.
8. **Logical Persuasion:** using data, statistics or expertise to persuade others.
9. **Coercion**: using threats or fear of punishment to get others to do what you want.

Develop Your Influence: Personal Exercise

Reflect on the nine strategies and then on your own preferred style. If it helps you, think about yourself in a particular situation where you have struggled to be influential.

Most-Used Strategy:

1) Why do you rely on this strategy so often?

2) When is it most effective?

3) In what situation(s) is this strategy not effective?

Future:

1) What strategies might you use more often in the future and why?

2) In what situations will these new strategies be most effective?

Exercise with a Mentor

Observe up to three influential leaders with whom you interact on a regular basis. Make note of what types of influence strategies they use most often and with what level of effectiveness. Create a journal with observations about:

1. The influential leader's name
2. Influence strategy used
3. Situation in which the strategy was used
4. Analysis of why the strategy was effective given the situation
5. Reflections about how and when use of the same strategy would be appropriate for you

Influencing in Service of Your Vision

I am going to circle us back to its beginning – to vision. Only this time, I'd like to suggest that you begin with personal vision and end, or better yet, incorporate along your life's journey, an opportunity for building shared vision. What is shared vision? It is a commonly held picture of a collectively desired future to which each person touched by it can feel a personal connection.

Shared vision is important because like personal vision, it provides directional force in our lives. It helps us anchor our energy to something positive and desirable. Remember, in the absence of a compelling vision, humans succumb to fear. And in the presence of fear, pettiness prevails—gossip, jealousy, apathy, self-deprecation. Shared vision focuses on how we might contribute to something larger than ourselves. When acted upon, we create something that is more powerful than we can bring into being alone. In the spirit of pursuing contribution, we lead and we follow others who are in sync with our desired for a better shared future.

Richard and I were recently invited to attend a gala sponsored by a young not-for-profit organization, he as a celebrity-host of the event and me as the President of the Make a Dent Foundation. Though we attend many charity events, this one was unique.

A lot of charities describe their good works, how the attendees' contributions have made a difference in the lives of others, and invite continued support. They are heart-wrenching and heart-warming experiences that always lead me to write a check. But the GEANCO Foundation's event was different. This gala opened with the unflinching declaration of a young woman, Nche Onyema, that she was building a hospital.

As the evening progressed, she and her siblings described growing up hearing stories of a promise made by their father, Godwin, to his father that he would one day return to Nigeria and build a hospital. Godwin's promise fueled his determination to obtain a medical degree then delay his return to Africa so that he could invest in the education of his own four children—at Princeton, Harvard, Georgetown and Boston College. "Wow" is right!

Godwin talked to his children and anyone else who would listen about his father's vision and his own promise. In the spring of that year, Godwin's second son, Afam, a graduate of Harvard University and Stanford Law School, declined multiple lucrative corporate law offers in order to work full-time to see his father's dream become a reality.

Today he serves as GEANCO's Chief Operating Officer and sits on the Foundation's board of directors with his brother, Gozie, and his sisters, Ebele and Nche. They serve together with respected and committed physicians, attorneys, business and healthcare management executives and high-level government officials who are all working tirelessly and passionately to ensure that promises made between fathers and sons are kept.

At the GEANCO gala, we were invited to join them in building a world-class hospital in Nigeria. We were invited into their vision and to share it. But here's the trick, they didn't sell us on a vision that was only important because it was handed down from grandfather to father to sons and daughters. Instead, they opened it up, created access points for everyone in attendance to see themselves as 1) compelled by the vision and 2) capable of contributing to its fulfillment.

How did they "open it up"? They started with values. They shared staggering statistics with us about life expectancy and infant mortality rates in Nigeria. They described how wealthy people leave the country to get world-class healthcare while the vast majority of people are being treated in facilities that would never be considered an option for even the poorest of Americans. They created a platform of shared values—basic care for children and poor people—and then called us to action. They gave us tangible ways to contribute and concrete language to acknowledge our effort: "I am building a hospital in Nigeria."

Here's the long view, shared vision fosters commitment over time. It engages you and others in an ecosystem where there is shared energy to grow and create—the eustress that allows movement toward a highly-anchored vision. Adaptive learning is possible without vision; that is, learning what not to do again or how to avoid unpleasant situations. But generative learning, actively making meaning and plans of action that make sense of experience and that respond to current realities, occurs only when people are striving to accomplish something that matters to them deeply.

It builds upon your existing <u>knowledge</u> with new <u>ideas</u> based on experimentation and open-mindedness, and allows you to find new way of viewing old, and perhaps, unsuccessful methods. Finally, shared vision provides a rudder for directional guidance, to keep the learning process on course when stresses develop. Learning can be difficult, even painful. With a shared vision we are more likely to expose our ways of thinking, give up deeply held views, and recognize personal responsibility and missteps that have gotten in our way in the past.

My last challenge to you: As you think about the next steps in your life's journey, consider :

1. Your potential contribution to something larger than yourself, and
2. What needs to move from the optional to the not-optional category in your mind to make it happen?

Now go do it! Just start moving, repeating your self-authoring talk with every step, and see where the journey takes you.

With the guidelines presented in this book, you'll find that your own destination can be as interesting, exciting and glamorous -- if you choose it to be -- as that of any "Housewife."

And here's the best part. No lights, cameras, close-ups or long-shots. Just a clear vision of a limitless future ahead – all episodes produced, written and directed by you.

Then "Watch What Happens"….

---

(1) Another amazing thing happens when you listen to the Universe: life fall beautifully into place. Turning my world upside down led, eventually, to me being reunited with a man I deeply love and who is the father of my son.

Epilogue

While working on the final draft of the manuscript for this book at home in Chicago, I watched—along with millions of others—as my life partner Richard Dent was announced as the NFL Hall of Famer and Super Bowl XX MVP who would be given the special ceremonial honor of conveying the Lombardi Trophy for presentation to the Baltimore Ravens, who had just become Super Bowl XLVII champions.

Richard sauntered onto the field, his baller swag still intact in his prestigious gold Hall of Famer jacket, basking in the stadium-wide showering of respect and affection by fans, his football peers and other NFL luminaries. Beyond my personal pride in his well-earned spotlight during the biggest sports event in America, I was immediately reminded of one of the major object lessons I am leaving with you in the pages of this book.

"Do you," he had advised me early on as I sought clarity on how to make all the pieces of my life fit. And his triumphant moment on the field of the New Orleans Superdome was a compelling testament to the power and enduring impact of "doing you" and doing it well. Through his prowess in football, Richard found a vehicle to give award-winning performances on the gridiron and in retirement, to play the game of life in an even more far-reaching way. He has used his celebrity to make a real difference—or a 'Dent' —by using his sphere of influence to do something for others larger than himself. And I am blessed to be a part of this rewarding effort through his Make a Dent Foundation.

I tell this story because you, too, can find your own vehicle to "do you" simply by putting in the work to identify and prioritize your goals, turn your passion into a marketable pursuit or just develop a more gratifying sense of self. Richard's support has reinforced my confidence that I could succeed by calling more of my own shots. And through his example of writing his own well-received memoir, *Blood, Sweat and Bears: Putting a Dent in the Game I Love,* Richard has inspired me to navigate these unknown waters of authorship myself.

In large part, I'm truly "doing me" because of him – the "me" carefully cultivated by overcoming my long struggle with identity, seeking out caring mentors who helped to strengthen my weaknesses, and acquiring the academic training and skill set that would enable me to go from being coached to coaching others around the world.

It is my sincere hope that this book will motivate and encourage other women to go beyond vicarious viewing of pop culture's camera-ready casts to achieve a more authentic and fulfilling life of your own.

Just imagine a 6-foot-5, 265-pound former NFL defensive end standing over your shoulder urging: "Do you!" And I guarantee, you will!

DeEtta Jones
Chicago, Illinois
February 2013

www.ingramcontent.com/pod-product-compliance
Lightning Source LLC
Chambersburg PA
CBHW040015240426
43664CB00036B/6